Conceptual
Self-Defense

Conceptual
Self-Defense

by

C. V. Rhoades

Turtle Press   Hartford

CONCEPTUAL SELF-DEFENSE

To contact the author or to order additional copies of this book:

    Turtle Press
    401 Silas Deane Hwy
    P.O. Box 290206
    Wethersfield, CT 06129-0206
    1-880-77-TURTL

ISBN 1-880336-54-5

Printed in the United States of America

NOTE TO READERS

Consult a physician before undertaking this or any other exercise regimen. Neither the author nor the publisher assumes any responsibility for the use or misuse of the information contained in this book.

Contents

Foreword 9
  Nurturing Our Natural Instincts 10
  Listening to Our Inner Voice 11
  Protecting Each Other 13

Attitude is Everything 15
  The Hard Facts of Crime 16
  Unique Concerns of Women 16
  Everything to Lose 18
  Honing Our Survival Instincts 20
  Making the Right Choices 24
  Getting Physical 27
  Don't Be There 30
  Martial Artists Share Their Philosophies 32
  Conquering Fear 34
  Controlling the Thought Process 38

Self-Defense and the Martial Arts 41
  The Role of Martial Arts In Self Defense 42
  Defining Self-Defense 44
  The Psychology of Martial Arts 46
  Choosing a Martial Art for Self-Defense 48
  The Benefits of Co-Ed Training 51
  Realistic Practice 52

Weapons: Pro and Con 55
  Weapons and Safety 57
  Seriousness of Intent 59
  Sprays and Stun Guns 60
  Woman's Best Friend 62
  Other Views on Weapons 62

A Special Message to Parents......................... 69

Techniques 71
   Avoidance Tactics...................................... 71
   Keep it Simple 73
   Hand Techniques...................................... 76
   Strikes 77
   Other Techniques 81
   Kicks and How to Use Them 83
   Targets 84
   Blocks 87
   Escapes 88
   Finding your Best Techniques 92

Scenarios 93
   Travel Safety 93
   Mental Practice...................................... 95

Overcoming Fear 101

   Bibliography.. 103
   About the Author 105

A quick thanks to my models:
Paul and Sabrina Rhoades, my children; my sister, Linda Lovato and my brother-in-law, Mike Lovato; and my niece and nephew, Shemmie and Judah Lovato.

Foreword

Self-defense is a matter of mind-set more than a matter of techniques.

In the animal kingdom, there are predators and prey. Predators depend on teeth, claws and speed to attack and kill their victims. Prey animals depend on their alertness and speed to escape, but are equipped with self-defense mechanisms that they can put to good use when threatened. Even a rabbit can kick with powerful hind legs and a duck can flail a dog with its wings.

Most animals, though, depend on being alert to threats, and to acting instinctively to what THEY PERCEIVE AS A THREAT. It doesn't have to be a real threat, even a perceived threat will cause a deer to bound away or a rabbit to head for his burrow. An animal will bolt from a photographer, who means them no harm, just as quickly as from a hunter with a rifle. They take no chances.

In *The Gift of Fear*, Gavin De Becker states, "Can you imagine an animal reacting to the gift of fear the way some people do, with annoyance and disdain instead of attention? No animal in the wild, suddenly overcome with fear, would spend any of its mental energy thinking, 'It's probably nothing.' They leave the scene first . . . Yet we chide ourselves for even momentarily giving validity to the feeling that ...someone's unusual behavior might be sinister." De Becker also points out that the root of the word intuition is 'tuere', which means, "to guard."

Animals depend on their sixth sense to tell them if there is a threat. African plains animals are always alert for lion attacks, but if the lions have recently eaten, they can walk right next to a herd of zebra and the zebra will continue grazing. The zebra can sense that the lions have no interest in hunting, so there is no reason to use precious energy fleeing every time they see a lion.

People too are born with this sixth sense, this instinct. In primitive cultures, people had to depend on finely honed survival instincts to survive. Wild animals and warring tribes presented threats to life, limb and family. With the coming of civilization, much of this was lost. We no longer had to worry about killer wild animals or outlaw gangs. Civilization brought law and order, sheriffs and police. We became complacent. We no longer looked inward to our own instincts for survival.

Even today, in American, most people feel "it won't happen to me." We have police forces, locks on our homes and cars, alarms and 911. We feel that we will be protected.

However, the police can't be everywhere. Violence is prevalent in many parts of the country. There are again violent gangs that rob, rape and murder for the thrill of it. There are serial killers. It is a jungle out there, filled not with chattering birds and monkeys, but killers with guns and knives. We should work to enhance our natural instincts for our own protection.

Nurturing Our Natural Instincts

Children often seem more in tune with this then do adults. Too often years of civilization dull this all-important instinct. Children are taught to obey adults without questioning; to be nice, even when their instincts tell them to leave; to let someone kiss or hug them when they feel uncomfortable about it; to be "good children" which often means quiet and conforming. Children are even taught not to speak their real feelings. How many times, as a child, were you hushed for saving something truthful, like, "Mom, that lady is fat," or "Mom, that man has a funny hat?" It may not be the socially acceptable thing to say, but it is the truth as they see it.

We should be very careful with our youngsters, not to destroy their belief in their senses.

As a self-defense mechanism, children should not be forced to kiss "Old Auntie Jane" or "Old Uncle Bill" if that adult makes them uncomfortable. When we force them to go against this feeling, we are training them not to listen to their instincts.

If they tell you they do not like a relative, or babysitter, or friend, listen and question them gently, not with antagonism, as to why. They may not be able to articulate the exact reason, but don't discount their feelings. Change babysitters. If a relative or friend is in question, don't leave you child alone with that person. The person is probably alright, but what if the child is right? Isn't it better to err on the side of caution rather than hearing, often years later, that said babysitter or relative or friend had abused your child, whom you had the responsibility to protect.

In *Safe Homes, Safe Neighborhoods, Stopping Crime where you Live*, the authors state, "Parents can help children by encouraging them to trust their own instincts. If children are approached by someone and they sense danger, it is important that they pay attention to those feelings...." They add that sensing danger and getting away could save their lives. In the same book, children's self-esteem is stressed, saying that good self-esteem can help prevent a child's victimization. Like predators who prey on adults, children's predators look for victims who appear weak or lonely.

Debbie Leung, in *Self Defense, the Womanly Art of Self-Care, Intuition and Choice*, states, "Intuition is a very powerful self-defense tool...which most women and children possess. One way children express intuitive feelings...is to describe these as 'uh-oh feelings'. Encourage them to talk to others, especially adults...whenever they have that feeling."

If a child, especially a girl, grows up learning to trust her instincts, she is less likely to be a victim of rape or violent crime.

Listening to Our Inner Voice

How many times have you felt that something about a person or situation wasn't right? How often did you act on that feeling? Feelings and instincts are our protection. Listen to your inner voice. Like the animals, if you perceive there is a threat, act on that, even if you may be wrong. Is it not better to wait a minute for the next elevator car, if the lone occupant makes you uncomfortable, than to take a chance that he might be a threat?

You may never know if your instincts were right, but why take a chance? Many times I have read of women who have been raped, or people who have been attacked, who later said, "I knew something was wrong. The whole thing didn't feel right." Yet they went against their feeling, their intuition, their better-judgement, and later wished they hadn't.

I often have intuitive feelings about various things. If I follow my intuition, I never know if it was correct. And yet, intuition has never led me into danger by following it. I would rather it be that way than have something tragic happen that I had literally foreseen.

In the animal world, the predator animals look for weak, sick, and easily killed prey. Human predators are the same way. They look for someone who is weak, scared, and easily subdued.

Sheepmen in the west have trouble with coyotes. They use dogs to herd the sheep, who don't get too excited upon seeing a coyote, which they think is just another dog. Sheep have few defenses and are easy prey.

Conversely, cattlemen are less affected by coyotes, as mother cows are more aggressive than mother sheep are. We raise longhorn cattle, who are by nature even more protective. Most have been left with their major defense weapon, their long, wicked horns, in fact. It would take an extremely foolish coyote or wolf to attack a longhorn cow protecting her calf. I once asked a fellow longhorn rancher if he had trouble with coyotes. He said, "No, and the neighbor's dogs take the long way around the pasture too."

Human predators act similarly. "Generally the attacker of today is a cowardly person," says Geoff Thompson in *Dead Or Alive, the Choice is Yours*. They look for weak, helpless victims who are less likely to do them harm. Human predators don't attack the strong or the fearless. They don't want to tie into someone that might hurt them instead.

Mike Lovato, a Clearmont, Wyoming self-defense instructor, told of a man he grew up with, and how he would walk along the street, sizing up victims. If they appeared weak, he would knock them down and grab their purses, or beat them up and rob them. But he sought out weak-appearing people.

Coyotes, like human predators, are cowardly but not dumb. How many coyotes are going to pass up a stupid, slow, meaty sheep in favor of a rabbit or antelope that they have to chase down before they can eat it? How many will pass up a tasty lamb in favor of a fawn or calf, when there is a chance that the mother will attack with hooves and horns? However, coyotes, being basically cowards, are not the most aggressive predators. Llamas are used by many to protect sheep, because llamas are not frightened of coyotes. They are curious and will walk up to a coyote. The coyote then slinks away, not wanting to attack prey that doesn't act afraid of it. Dogs are the same way. Let a cow or horse jump and take off in fear of a dog, and the dog will chase it. Let the same cow or horse approach the dog without fear and most dogs will slink away.

So it is with human predators. Is a wallet or a rape really worth the criminal's time if they know, or even perceive, that there will be a fight involved? Even acting differently from the norm, i.e., not frightened, will often deter attackers or rapists.

In the book *Dead or Alive*, Geoff Thompson talks about psyching the antagonist out and stopping his intended onslaught. "Not many people will enter into a confrontation if they think that there is a chance of them getting hurt," Thompson says. He relates a story of a world renowned Martial arts teacher, who was walking down a "quiet suburban street on his way home after his usual, nightly teaching session. He noticed three hoodlums hovering, several yards away on the opposite side of the street. When they approached him he was ready. 'Give us your money, or you'll get hurt,' said the leader of the three. Master Abbe looked at each one in turn, then casually took his wallet out of his jacket pocket, threw it on the floor between him and his antagonists. He pointed to the wallet and said, 'I'm prepared to die for that wallet. Are you?' The three would-be attackers looked at the wallet...then at Abbe, then at each other. Without further ado they all ran away, obviously not prepared to die for the wallet. Master Abbe picked up his wallet and calmly walked home."

Protecting Each Other

Often in nature, especially in wild cattle, deer and horses, one bleat of a baby animal will bring not only the mother but the entire herd to defend the youngster. Muskox, when attacked by wolves, form a circle of defense, putting the sick and weak and young in the center with the mature, healthy members around the outside, heads down, to fight off the attacking predators.

Several hunters have experienced moose defending a dead comrade. And American Bison go crazy if blood is scented: the entire herd of animals, each weighing over a thousand pounds, converge around the spot, ready to do major battle with whomever is injuring one of 'their own.'

It is too bad that much of human society has lost the protective instinct toward their own kind. Small towns still have this. People know each other, are interested in each other. Kids can walk the streets safely and if your youngster is missing, you simply call all your neighbors until you find where he/she is. We still watch out for each other, and crime rates in small towns are low.

Perhaps society, as a whole, is too dependent upon the police and courts to protect us. I think its time to take the initiative to protect ourselves. Police can't be everywhere at once, and citizens have to take more responsibility for their own safety, and the safety of their neighborhoods. That's why neighborhood watch programs are a crime deterrent. Neighbors watch out for each other.

Mark Carey is one of the pioneers of the restorative justice program in Minnesota. In a speech in Sheridan, Wyoming in 1999, Carey quoted John Braithwaite, author of *Crime, Shame and Reintegration,* in saying, "Low crime societies are societies where everyone doesn't mind their own business, but are interested in each other."

There seems to be more of the "watch out for your neighbor" mind-set in rural areas, where police are far away. Because of this, we use common sense when it comes to self-defense.

Taking the concept further, Gerald Blanchard, licensed professional counselor, talks about restorative justice. He said "In Canada, they use the Native Canadian model of circle healing and sacred justice. It involves the community and trained volunteers within the community to help both victim and perpetrator."

Carey said the program has been successful in one Minnesota county for six years. He is encouraging other communities to look into the concept as a way to help control crime.

But, everyone can do their part in their own neighborhoods. If someone is being hurt, get involved, call the police. Low crime societies result when everyone gets involved with everyone else.

Many animals band together for protection. They protect themselves, their young, and each other. Each member of the herd is valuable. So it should be with humans.

In self-defense, the first, very first, key is attitude. Don't be a prey animal. Be that caribou in the herd that looks the wolf straight in the eye, stomps his feet, snorts through his fuzzy nose, and says, "Ok, boy, come and get me, but expect a fight and a few bleeding wounds and bruises. Come on, if you think you are man enough." The wolf, unless he is rabid or extremely hungry, will slink off in search of weaker prey.

We want to be that caribou.

Chapter 1

Attitude is Everything

Develop a strong attitude, a warrior bearing.

Some people seem to be born with this attitude, what I prefer to call the survival instinct, rather than killer instinct. Some writers say it cannot be taught, but I feel that to a certain extent, it can.

You have to maintain a good self-image. In being self-confident, a person shows strength. In old Japan, a master of the tea ceremony once accidentally insulted a samurai. Angrily, the samurai challenged the tea master to a duel. Frightened, the tea master asked a famous swordsman for help. The tea master was hopelessly inept with the sword, and finally the swordsman gave up, telling the man he would die. Then, to calm the man, he asked him to make tea. The swordsman, watching him make the tea, told him, "Do tomorrow like you are doing now. Your mind is empty. You neither desire life nor fear death. When your enemy attacks tomorrow, raise the sword above your head, and be prepared to cut and die."

The next day, following the swordsman's advice, the tea master was waiting calmly, without fear, for the samurai. The samurai, seeing no fear, turned and walked away.

The Hard Facts of Crime

Today, you don't have to be paranoid to worry about violent crime. It is all around us, especially for women. Statistically, three out of four women will be a victim of violent crime. According to the U.S. Department of Justice figures for 1998, there were an "estimated 1.5 million violent crimes. That is a rate of 556 violent crimes per every 100,000 inhabitants. Data collected on weapons used in connection with violent crimes showed personal weapons, (hands, fists and feet), were used in 31 percent of all murders, robberies and aggravated assaults." To us, this means that in about one third of all attacks, we only have to worry about someone attacking us with their hands or feet, not with weapons.

According to the same statistics, "Firearms were used in 25 percent of violent crimes; knives or cutting instruments in 15 percent and other dangerous weapons were involved in 28 percent." The Justice Department reports that six out of ten reported murders were committed with a firearm. There is a section in the book on how to avoid being a statistic of a firearm related encounter.

Aggravated assault accounted for 64 percent of all violent crimes, with an estimated 974,402 aggravated assaults being reported. Murder accounted for only one percent. Robbery made up 29 percent. So, according to statistics, we have a fairly good chance of escaping being killed. In fact, the number of murders dropped from 1997 to 1998 by seven percent. The murder rate of six offenses per 100,000 inhabitants was the lowest figure since 1967. There were 17,000 estimated murders in 1998. Seventy-six percent of murder victims were male.

Although 76 percent of the murder victims are male, among female murder victims, a whopping 32 percent were slain by husbands and boyfriends, while only four percent of the male murder victims were slain by their wives or girlfriends.

Unique Concerns of Women

If you are a woman, there is a good chance, if you are a victim, you will be a victim of an assault committed by someone you know. Many times it is someone you love and trust. While addressing the domestic violence issue would require an entire book, women who increase their self-esteem are less likely to be victims of domestic violence, by marrying a battering spouse for example, and less likely to let the cycle continue once it begins.

There were 93,103 estimated forcible rapes reported to law enforcement during 1998. Although it was the lowest total in a decade, it is still very high, with 67 out of 100,000 females in the country becoming victims of rape.

Although the figures, according to the Justice Department, have dropped from 1997 to 1998, they are still enough to make one think about personal safety. That is what this book is about. Although its concepts are applicable for women and men, boys and girls, the main thrust of the book is for women who want to learn ways and means to defend themselves. Women are very often raised in ways that contribute to being a victim.

A friend and I were one day discussing sexual abuse of children. Both of us had been raised with the current philosophies of the time, Terry, during the 30s and myself during the 50s. Looking back, we knew that, as children, we would have been prime targets because we were raised to be polite, nice and little ladies. Most girls, even today, are raised according to these standards.

The age old question, are women naturally less aggressive or have they been trained to be less aggressive, may never be answered. The nature versus nurture theory is still being debated by the best minds in the country. It is probably a little of both. Women, by nature, are nurturers, while men are protectors. In my own case, I was raised to be less aggressive, at least my mom tried. My father, with whom I spent most of my time, urged me to quit 'working like a girl' and to 'work like a man.' I was thankful for his intervention to keep me from being a 'little lady.' I was and still am a very physically active and assertive person, mostly due to his influence.

Although modern Western society perpetrates the myth of a soft, non-aggressive woman, there have been several societies where women were more aggressive. They were accepted and their fighting talents utilized.

Various Indian tribes had women warriors, highly respected in the tribe and capable of fighting alongside the men. One Apache woman, Lozen, the younger sister of Victorio, one of the leaders of the band, was a skilled archer and horsewoman. Victorio one said, "Lozen is as my right hand. Strong as a man, braver than most, and cunning in strategy."

In Native American cultures, the roles were not as sharply defined as in many white cultures. *The Woman's Way* states, "Females could take on the responsibilities of men if they wished and visa versa. Thus, on occasion, Indian women served as hunters, scouts, diplomats and even warriors."

As a case in point, a Cheyenne woman, Buffalo-Calf-Road-Woman, fought beside her husband, Black Coyote, in the Battle of the Rosebud in Montana. When her brother was surrounded by Crow scouts from General Crook's calvary, she raced her pony to his side, rescuing him from the enemy. The Cheyenne's call the battle, The Fight Where the Girl Saved Her Brother. Another Indian woman fought against Custer at the Battle of the Little Bighorn, which was fought a week later.

Historically, many women have fought in wars and lead armies. Sara Emma Edmonds, who, disguised as a man, fought in the Civil War; Joan of Arc and Queen Boadicea who lead armies; Qui Jin who was a poet, equestrian and swordswoman, and a member of a revolutionary Chinese organization, are just a few "warrior women." If they can do it, surely each of us can protect ourselves and our families against present day threats.

We know that female animals can be very ferocious in protection of their young. In fact, animals have more respect for the ferocity and fighting spirit of a mother protecting her young than humans do. A boar bear will kill a cub, but will back down from a female who is protecting her young, even though the boar could overcome the female. He knows that, in protection of her young, the female will deal a lot of damage. Animals also seem to respect the fact that the female is fighting for her offspring.

If you have children, wouldn't you go all-out to protect them from a threat and do whatever it might take to stop the attack?

Everything to Lose

If you are threatened, remember, your family needs you back. In protecting yourself, you are protecting your children from a life that they may have to live without you, if you should be killed. Think about life on these terms.

A friend once said, it a weak moment I'm sure, because I doubt that he believes it now, "I wouldn't kill someone in self-defense. What makes my life more important than his?"

To my mind this is backwards thinking. Anyone who preys on another deserves what he gets, i.e., possibly being killed. Your life may not be worth more than his, if this is your thinking, but maybe the next person he tries to kill feels his or her life is much more important. If you are in a situation where you have to choose between your life and your attacker's, remember, you are probably not the first, and you won't be the last. You are saving not only your own life, (whether you feel it worth anything or not,) but you may be saving the life of someone else. Does this make the whole issue seem more worthwhile?

For effective self-defense, we have to harness this instinct to be used to protect the most important person at the time of an attack, YOURSELF.

In *Beauty Bites Beast* by Ellen Snortland, she mentions that females have few, if any, role models today to show them how to be a warrior. Most television shows, with the exception of *Xena, Warrior Princess*, show women as being protected and saved by men. The media does not show women defending themselves, or taking the initiative in a confrontation. This is too bad. We should have strong role models, just as men do. Boys have James Bond, John Wayne, Clint Eastwood, Charles Bronson, and a host of others who can take care of themselves in any imagined circumstance.

Young girls need more strong women characters to emulate. Girls should be encouraged to read about strong women, even those who went outside the norm of their society, such as Calamity Jane, Carrie Nation, Charlie (Charlotte) Parkenhurst, and Belle Starr, all strong woman, who followed their own paths and convictions. In my own case, growing up on a ranch and going to John Wayne movies whenever they came to the drive-in, I made John Wayne and others my role models. Heck with the fact that I was a woman. I could ride, brand and shoot with the best of my screen heros. I still can. It would have been nice, though, to have movies about strong women to identify with and incorporate into my persona.

I especially liked in Snortland's book a segment about puppies. From birth, puppies roll and tumble, growl and nip, bite and tug in play. These are all acts that an adult dog, male and female, uses for taking prey or protecting themselves, their territory, or their young. The same is true with cats, horses and cows. The play-actions of the young are the same acts the adult animal uses in later life to survive.

Think how our young women are taught. We are not taught to fight. Young boys are encouraged to be rough and tumble, to proclaim their masculinity with their fists. Young girls are taught to be nice, to sit and watch, and to not spoil our dresses. Hum. Makes one think. If we trained our young girls to be assertive, even aggressive, perhaps the balance of power between the sexes would even out.

Honing Our Survival Instincts

Back to the survival instinct. How does one develop it? Survival is usually not a matter of skillful techniques, although these can help if the situation deteriorates to a life-or-death matter. Survival is a finely tuned extra-sensory feeling, an attitude of "I'm important, I respect myself, and I won't give in to intimidation or violence."

There are many examples of this type of attitude that can be found in both Eastern and Western literature. One of my favorites is the following story from Japan.

Yagyu Tajima-no-kami was a great swordsman in the shogun's court. He was asked by one guard to give the guard training in fencing. Yagyu Tajima-no-kami told the guard that he could tell that the guard was already a master, but the guard denied knowing anything. Still, the teacher was sure that the man knew more than he was letting on. "I know you are a master of something," Yagyu told the guard.

"I will tell you," the guardsman said. "When I was still a boy, the thought came to me that as a samurai I ought in no circumstances to be afraid of death, and I have grappled with the problem of death for some years now, and finally the problem of death has ceased to worry me. May this be what you sense?"

"Exactly," exclaimed Tajima-no-kami. He told the guard that the ultimate secrets of swordsmanship lie in being released from the thought of death. "You need no technical training. You are already a master."

In Native American culture, the warriors, before going into battle, often said among themselves, "It is a good day to die," In this way they were embracing the possibly of death, and were not afraid of it.

In the Old West, some of the deadliest killers were those who had nothing to lose. Doc Holliday, who knew for years he was dying of tuberculous, didn't really give a damn. In fact, he would have probably relished going out in a gun battle, rather than dying, as he did, in a hospital. However, his willingness to face death probably made him live longer than he otherwise would have.

To put this attitude into an analogy that most of us can relate to, have you ever tried to avoid something, only to make it worse? And have it happen anyway. Think of a car in a bad skid. How many of us panic and hit the brakes, making the skid worse? One day I was riding with a friend who nearly hit a deer. She over-reacted, steering wildly, and ran off the road. Had she not panicked, she probably would have stayed on the road. Maybe in a life-or-death situation, this could be put into practice. Don't panic and make a wrong move. If you do not become overwhelmed by fear, you can retain a calmer demeanor, and often this may be enough to save your life.

Revered Chinese philosopher Lao Tzu once said, "He who knows how to live can walk abroad without fear of rhinoceros or tiger. He will not be wounded in battle, for in him rhinoceroses can find no place to thrust their horn, tigers no place to use their claws, and weapons no place to pierce. Why is this so? Because he has no place for death to enter." I think there is a lot to be said for this attitude.

One man I interviewed in 1997 was the last survivor of World War I living in our town. He was close to 100 years old still lived alone at home, and was alert and lively for his age. He told me, "I made it through World War I. I figured if that didn't kill me, nothing would." He had a good attitude on life.

In my own case, I have been close to death twice. Once in a car accident where I had a near-death experience of going towards a bright circle of light and once in a horse accident where the doctor told me later he thought I was a goner a couple of times. Based on these experiences, I can see nothing to fear from death. I don't want to die, but the thought doesn't bother me. We all have to go sometime.

However, having said that, I won't accept my death at the hands of someone else without putting up a fight. I intend if I ever (God forbid) find myself in a life or death situation, to take someone out with me when I go, or at least deal some intensive damage in the process. By not fearing death, I can fight to the finish. I don't want to give in easily.

There was once a newscast about an elderly lady who witnessed a man raping a young girl. The older lady, with rocks and sticks, attacked the rapist and drove him off. "Look for him in the emergency room," she told police. He was found and arrested.

Often, such decisions are made without conscious thought. The lady probably didn't waste time thinking that she could be hurt, she simply did what she had to do. This is the attitude we want to cultivate. The attitude of no fear.

Women are most vulnerable and are more concerned about personal safety due to the violence against women in our society.

Rape is overwhelmingly a woman's concern. Men and boys are raped, but the percentage is small compared to women. There are conflicting books on the subject of what to do if confronted by a rapist. Some say "fight your hardest", some say, "give in and enjoy it" (these, hopefully, are being struck from every library shelf,) some say, "fight only if your life is threatened," (I wonder how many men would follow this advice?) some say, "try to talk to them," (some are so far gone on drugs or alcohol, that they won't listen), etc. There are as many different ideas as there are people who may use them. So what should you really do? The best thing is to be aware, keep calm and be ready for what you decide is the right action at any given time. Each case is different, so everyone has to react differently, and no one approach will work in all situations. There is a big difference between a single attacker and multiple attackers. There is a difference between being confronted by someone who is looking for cheap thrills and someone who is a hardened criminal with a desire to kill someone. Often, your instincts will guide you if you stay calm and listen to the inner voice. The most important thing is to STAY CALM.

One of the best books I have seen on the subject is *The Gift of Fear*. In this book the author encourages people to use their instincts. If you think a situation is dangerous, you are probably right. Over and over again in self-defense classes, books and women's support groups, the phase 'use your instinct' is brought up again and again, and yet women have been attacked by people they felt uncomfortable with. Often, to avoid hurting the man's feelings, they didn't listen to this little inner voice that said, "Hey, something isn't right here."

Mike Lovato says, "Legally, self-defense, especially for a woman, depends on the perception of the defender. If you think the situation warrants excessive force, it probably does. In self-defense, we don't train people to be paranoid and think that everyone is out to get them, but you have to be prepared.

"Self defense teaches you to be proactive, and to approach situations warily. Self-defense teaches you how to keep it at a distance, but also how to react when that distance is closed."

I am a big believer in watching nature's interplay, and a lot can be learned from it. I grew up on a ranch, and learned from animals several ways of relating that can be transferred to the world of humans. A good bluff is often all that is necessary. Even cattle, larger, stronger and faster than humans, can often, not always, be bluffed into believing that a puny human can conquer them. They like to try to bluff us as well. A cow will snort, paw the ground, and put on a display to say, "Hey, I'm tough. Stay away." Usually, though, if you run at them and swing a big stick, they will run. But you have to be bold and decisive. You have to be ready to slap that cow across the nose with the stick if she doesn't run. (My brother-in-law, who is a black belt in Kempo, uses a wooden sword. He says they don't break as easy on a cow's head as sticks do.) When working cows, I do my homework. I have an escape route, a fence to climb on in case my bluff doesn't work. But I have learned to not be afraid, to think, "Okay, if she runs at me instead of away from me, can I get on the fence?" This is not a panic response, this is a well-planned defense. Even generals in a war usually have a retreat route planned in case they need to back out of an offensive.

Remember the prey animals, too. They run at a PERCEIVED threat. They don't question. They don't wonder if their instincts are right. They don't wait to see if you are friend or foe. Occasionally, ranch horses pull this same trick. Even though they know you, know you will feed them, and know you won't hurt them, they pretend you are the most menacing thing on the face of the earth. They kick up their heels and run off into the pasture. They leave if they think there is a threat. This can apply to humans. There are many situations where, even if there is no threat, it is better to avoid it. If you are alone at night, and see a group of men walking toward you, and feel they might cause trouble, you should simply find a way to get out of the situation before you are in the middle of something bad. Like a deer, flee from the situation.

Deer depend on speed, but also on stealth. I have seen very large buck deer sneak down draws, quietly, walking away without a sound, usually without the hunter even being aware that they were there. That is what you have to do when threatened.

If you have a place to run to, it is best to leave a situation quietly, hopefully before anyone even takes notice of you.

You can practice ways to make yourself practically invisible. Simply stop and let yourself blend in with your surroundings.

Making the Right Choices

In *Self Defense, The Womanly Art of Self-care, Intuition and Choice,* Debbie Leuge states, "Self-defense is a way of nurturing ourselves by caring about our own safety and the safety of others. It involves intuition and making choices."

This is what I do when I'm in big cities, such as Denver. I make sure the car doors are locked, and that my money is on my person, not swinging in a shoulder purse. I stay out of the rougher sections of town. I keep my motel room locked, and am careful whom i let in the door. These are all common sense, safety precautions. Once I have taken precautions, I enjoy myself. I don't always worry, "Oh my God, I'm going to be mugged." I walk with confidence and assurance, and I map out where I am going in advance. In knowing where I am going and how to get there, I gain confidence. That confidence comes across to others. Even if I don't know where I am, or where I am going, I act as if I do. Who is going to know? I don't let anyone see that I am insecure.

When in London a couple of years ago, our guide, a friend, told us to "carry only what money you'll need, carry it in a pocket or in something close to your body. Don't wear flashy jewelry." When she walked, it was fast and purposeful, hardly looking around. She purchased a map so she would know where to go, and we followed her for a whirlwind tour. Nothing happened, but I would not be willing go into London without someone who knew the ropes. It is a huge city, and I know I could easily get lost.

Sometimes, staying safe is a matter of knowing your limitations, whether it is not going somewhere you are unfamiliar with or not getting into a situation where your physical skills may be vastly inferior. For one thing, confidence is a big deterrent against crime, and if you feel out-of-your-element, you won't be as confident.

Here is where you listen to your intuition. I would not walk the streets of London or Denver and feel completely safe. I would always be in an alert mode.

In my own hometown, I can walk without fear. I'm still alert, but not to the same degree. It is the difference between driving on an open highway and driving on a three-lane interstate at rush hour. The degree of alertness is much different.

I also liken alertness to the difference between riding an old, well-trained ranch gelding and a young horse that is in training. Both are horses, but the old ranch gelding is unlikely to spook much, or suddenly decide to buck. You can jog along, talk to your partner, watch the sky and the deer on the hillsides, and enjoy the ride. The saddle creaks, the reins lay easy on the horse's neck. Very little guidance is necessary, and the horse and I are both relaxed and calm.

When riding a young horse, I am at all times "listening" to the horse beneath me with my body. I can feel his muscles tense, I watch his ears swivel back and forth. I can never really relax and enjoy the ride, I have to be aware of the youngster I am riding, and be ready to deal with the horse's reactions to the new, exciting and often scary realities of learning to be a safe, dependable mount. It is necessary to be alert, but not frightened or nervous. If I'm nervous, the horse senses it and feels frightened. I have to project a calm, secure feeling. They can sense fear, and sense when a rider is not confident. In a horse/rider relationship, confidence builds confidence. If you are confident of your riding skills, this is communicated to the horse, and he, in turn, knows he can trust you, and he feels confident in you.

For some reason, this can also be sensed by humans. If you have ever listened to a person making a speech when they are scared to death, you can tell that they are scared the minute you see them on the stage. Human predators are very adept at reading these signs of fear and nervousness in their intended victims.

The creator gave us our inner voice. I'm sure the caveman listened to this voice when a cave bear growled inside a cave, or warned them away from the berry patch. I'm pretty sure that they listened to that inner voice when a saber-toothed cat came by, smelling a fresh kill and wanting his share. Did they invite him in by the fire? Not likely. That little inner voice said, "Hey, this animal has long teeth and sharp claws. Sure, his feelings will be hurt if you throw that rock. His head will hurt too, but he may not come back and eat you for supper along with your fresh kill."

A wolf, one of nature's best prey animals, knows that he is facing death each time he runs to drag down a healthy caribou or moose. A moose's hoof can cleave the wolf's skull. A caribou's horns and hooves can deal damage. Likewise, a human predator knows, or should know, that any time he attacks another human, he could be hurt and/or killed. One time I read about a string of laundromats that were being held up in Texas. One police chief had a unique plan to curtail the robberies. He put an armed guard in few select laundromats, and spread the word on the street. Any robber would be playing Russian roulette. If he went to rob the laundry, there may be a man behind the counter with a shot gun, ready to shoot. The robberies dropped off.

There is a story about a woman who picked up a cold, frozen snake, warmed it up and brought it back to life, then complained when the snake bit her. The snake said, "Hey, you knew I was a snake when you brought me home."

We have to accept that some people out there are snakes. Some are out-and-out bad. Don't encourage these people. Don't worry about hurting their feelings. Don't worry about hurting their heads, if it comes to that.

Often, in life, as in sports such as basketball, the best defense is a good offense. Robin Buckingham echoes the sentiment. "First off, simply don't be there. Don't put yourself in a situation where you might have to use self-defense," she says.

Like she says, don't be there. Assess the situation. In Basic Emergency Care Classes, we are taught, before offering help, to assess the situation for danger. Decide if you really want to go into that bar or take that shortcut through a dark alley. Make the choice; make it a safe one. It is easier and smarter to set up a good offense, rather than to have be defensive.

In Thompson's book, he talks about the "mad man/woman" approach, where by becoming loud and aggressive one came sometimes make the attacker feel he has bitten off more than he can chew if he tangles with you. As an added bonus, being aggressive can often draw attention to you and the situation, perhaps from someone who will help.

Getting Physical

Unfortunately, women are likely to raped not only by strangers, where learning the self-defense techniques and doing them with speed and determination can possibly stop the altercation, but also by men they know.

One friend of mine is having trouble with her very large son, as he often refuses to respect her. He is not violent, but he laughs at her attempts to discipline him. She wants to learn some techniques that would allow her to, basically, show him she can't be intimated without really hurting him. However, this respect should have started when the boy was very young. Just like a young horse who learns that bucking and kicking and biting only gets him popped with a whip, young children have to learn respect early, not after they have achieved their full growth.

Often, some physical skills are needed though: A way to diffuse a situation, say with a drunken date who won't take no for and answer, allowing the woman to remain in control of the situation without really hurting them. This could be a technique such as joint lock, choke, or pressure points strike, made to disable for a time but not do extensive damage. In a perfect world, we would be able to perceive the danger before getting into a situation where self-defense is necessary, but this is not a perfect world. We have to live with what we have, and learn how to not only avoid the situation, but also HOW TO PROTECT OURSELVES SHOULD THE SITUATION ARISE.

If a situation is just beginning, say a man is talking to you and you don't want anything to do with him, you can use several techniques: the tight lipped smile, turning away, ignoring him. Just walking away can often end the situation before it starts. Many assailants are good at disarming the victim by appearing to be a nice guy, appearing helpful and considerate. Both Thompson's book and de Becker's give examples of women who were raped and/or killed by people who were skilled at deception. This is when following your instinct comes in to play. De Becker says, "Every day people engaged in the clever defiance of their own intuition become, in mid thought, victims of violence and accidents.

"A woman could offer no greater cooperation to her soon-to-be attacker than to spend time telling herself, 'but he seems like such a nice man.'" de Becker continues. Many women are more afraid of INSULTING a person by, say, not getting into an elevator with a man when their instinct clearly tells them to wait for the next car, then they are for THEIR OWN SAFETY.

On the Dr. Laura Schlessinger show, she often expresses amazement at callers who let others hurt their feelings, and don't fight back for fear of hurting the other person's feelings, making the other person more important than themselves.

I live in Wyoming, where much of the culture revolves around bars and drinking. I don't like to go into a bar, even our local bar, at night when there are a lot of people who have been drinking for sometime, even though I know nearly everyone there. If I do have to go in, I make it a point to be in and out quickly, but without acting afraid. I let my eyes sweep the room, speaking to those customers whom I know, and basically ignoring or responding lightly to the smart remarks that many of the men make. Most of the time I joke and smile with them, as I know they mean no harm. But if I feel that they are over the line on anything, I simply turn away and go about my business of buying pop or whatever and leave. I'm not afraid, but I also don't let them intimidate me, or let someone I don't feel comfortable around pull me into a conversation. I DON'T WORRY ABOUT BEING THOUGHT OF AS A SNOB OR A BITCH. I DON'T CARE IF I HURT SOMEONE'S FEELINGS. THEY WILL HEAL.

That is their problem. I have the right to choose who I talk to. Just because they want to talk to me, doesn't give them the right to force their conversation, or anything else, on me. I have the freedom to choose. Usually, my best choice is to stay out of the bar when I know that there will be drunk people there. I have never had a problem in our local bars, but there was one bar, now closed and gone, where I never felt comfortable, and refused to go into, even to buy a Coke. It just felt bad. I'll never know if my feelings saved me from an unpleasant confrontation, but they may have. I'm just as glad not to know.

A woman I work with used to own a bar and served the drinkers in the evening. One evening a regular customer was there and a man that my friend didn't know walked in. She immediately felt that he was dangerous, and asked the regular customer to stay until closing time and take her home. He did, and nothing happened. Would something have happened if she had ignored her inner voice? Maybe. Luckily, she didn't ignore it and all turned out well.

One self-defense class instructor put it this way, "Avoid bars, people who drink heavily or do drugs, regardless of who they are. These are all negative energies."

Society has to change in how we perceive women before there is real equality, but until this happens, we, as women or others who may feel intimidated, have to take the initiative by showing those who would prey on us that we are not easy prey. We have to train ourselves and our daughters to be more powerful. We have to remember that our intuition is often right, and that no one's feelings are more important than our safety. Remember when your feelings were hurt? You got over it. It did not bruise, it did not require hospitalization. Feelings do heal.

Often, the trauma of rape does not. Although many people deride the "Looking out for Number One" philosophy, we have to look out for ourselves first. In fact, I am taking a course on Basic Emergency Care designed to train people to be First Responders in traumas such as car wrecks, heart attacks and strokes. The teacher stresses that you, as the responder, must take care of yourself. Assess the scene, if it is not safe, do not go in. "A dead rescuer is no rescuer," is our reoccurring theme. If you are on a scene, and your partner is hurt, take care of the partner before you take care of the victim. Therefore, your first responsibility is yourself, then your partner, then the person who needs help. This is the same in self-defense. You are the most important person to keep alive.

If you are gone, or hurt, you not only suffer, but your children, your parents, your spouse, and your friends suffer as well. If you don't fight back for yourself, do it for those who depend on you.

The old cliche, "an ounce of prevention is worth a pound of cure" is applicable here. Do not put yourself in a bad situation. It is easier to avoid confrontation than have to defend yourself.

In *Instructors Guide to Teaching Women Self-Defense Seminars*, Brian J. Olden, says that "Recent statistics from the U.S. Department of Justice indicate that there are a number of effective strategies that can be used by women when faced with an attack."

Women have....
"Resisted or captured the attacker.
Scared or warned the offender;
Persuaded or appeased the offender;
Ran away and hid;
Attacked the offender;
Screamed, sounded an alarm or got help."

Olden suggests that even if the attacker has a weapon, flight is still the best response. "In a recent article, an author analyzed the process of firing a gun and found that an error of only five degrees in pointing a firearm will result in a miss."

As a hunter, I know that it is very easy to miss, even with a scope. With an open sight, such as most pistols have, hitting a target is even more difficult, especially a moving, zigzagging target. Olden says, "His (the writer) conclusion, was that the majority of people carrying a weapon, such as a gun, are poorly trained in its use. The reason these weapon-wielding assailants are often successful is because of THE FEAR CAUSED BY THE SIGHT OF THE WEAPON." All women should take a course in the use of firearms. For one thing, just finding out how a firearm works can eliminate some of this fear.

Don't Be There

Self defense is not just one set of techniques or one philosophy, but most instructors stress avoidance and assessment of a situation, calmness, confidence and courage. Self-defense, like martial arts, covers a wide variety of self-protective skills. Look in any martial arts magazine, and there are advertisements for self-protection videos and books teaching techniques used by Navy Seals, bodyguards and other experts.

Every instructor has their own ideas on what works, and what they stress in their classes. In talking to several instructors, martial artists and police on the topic of self-defense, I found each recommended a slightly different way of dealing with trouble. However, as much as they differ in techniques and training, they agree on the most important point in self-defense: DON'T BE THERE IN THE FIRST PLACE.

Buckingham feels the biggest problem is that most people feel, "It won't happen to me. People need to think more about self-defense. We lock our homes and our cars, but we don't think about protecting ourselves. People should pay more attention to protecting themselves."

This is a telling point. We are a possession oriented society. A man will often do more time in jail for stealing something, than they will for harming someone. It seems as if we value money and things more than life itself, a rather backwards way of looking at things. We worry more about protecting our property than our own lives.

There is an old joke about a stingy man who was confronted by a robber. "Your money or your life," the man demanded. After long and careful thought, the stingy man said, "Take me life, I'm saving me money for me old age." Self defense was not a high priority for him.

Melissa Horton, instructor at the Jade Forest Kung Fu studio in Rapid City puts it this way, "We teach self-defense as a part of learning practice. We incorporate self-defense in kung fu, as well as teaching specific applications. We teach awareness and focus."

Her philosophy is, "The best defense is not to be in a confrontational situation. Defuse the situation and then leave. If you cannot get away, then fight. I believe in being honorable and smart." Many martial arts schools focus on the same philosophy: defusing the situation, being aware of your surroundings, being honorable and smart. When I read about many women who were attacked or raped, it seemed as if they were just plain not paying attention, and weren't being very smart about their choices. However, like my father always said, "hindsight is 20/20." He was right. We can all look back on events and know, after the fact, what we would have done differently.

Being aware of your surroundings is what law enforcement officers are taught. David Hein, police officer in Sheridan, Wyoming, said, "In law enforcement, we have three levels of awareness of your environment. White: that means you feel safe. You are not aware of what is going on around you, you might be deep in thought. You're not paying attention. Yellow: you are alert and aware. You know about a guy standing by a stop light, you know if someone falls in behind you on the sidewalk. You are not frightened, but you are aware. Red is an actual threat. Red means you are ready to survive, ready to fight if necessary."

Mike Lovato also added black for panic. "Panic is where you don't want to be. That is as bad as white. You should act before you get to the panic stage."

Always remember, no matter what the situation is, don't panic. Panic interferes with clear thinking, and should be avoided in all situations.

Martial Artists Share Their Philosophies on Self-Defense

In doing the book, I was curious as to what others had to say. I wanted to see how much was similar as well as how the various instructors differed in their approaches to self-defense. I have included some of the information I gathered in this section. I feel you can learn something from everyone, taking what you feel works for you and discarding the rest.

Sifu John Loupos

Sifu John Loupos is the owner of the Jade Forest Kung Fu/Tai Chi/Internal Arts in Cohasset, Mass. He has been involved in the martial arts since 1966. He has been teaching martial arts since 1968, as he puts it, "Curious and serendipitous events left me with my own school at the tender age of 15 back in 1968. I have been teaching martial arts ever since."

Sifu Loupos said of self defense, "All life is sacred, including your own. In pursuing a study of martial arts we assume a self appointed obligation to learn how to protect ourselves when encroached upon by another person or persons. Should the occasion arise we must inflict no more harm than is necessary to secure our own safety. By the same measure we must do no less than is necessary to remain just as safe."

This is why we should, if at all possible, diffuse the situation before it becomes physical. That way, avoiding the confrontation, we don't get hurt, nor does anyone else.

Mike Lovato

Mike Lovato, who has taught self-defense workshops in Buffalo and Clearmont, has been in martial arts "a lifetime. We all, my brothers and sisters and I, started when my cousin taught us military ju-jitsu. He was the instructor for the WWII paratroopers. I have been a martial arts instructor for about 6 years. But I have taught many people informally."

His self-defense philosophy, gained from the military and from growing up in rough neighborhoods is, "Avoid a physical confrontation if possible; if not, hit first, hit hard, fast and furiously."

He calls his self defense techniques Swift, Silent and Deadly. "You need to be fast, you don't want them to know its coming and it has be to forceful."

If you choose to use a self-defense technique, be prepared to go all the way, using enough force to allow yourself an opportunity to get away. Don't do it half way, you're running the risk of just making your opponent madder. For one thing, you've given yourself away. He knows now that, whatever you do, you don't really mean it. It's just like saying 'No' and then giggling. Is it really serious? When you say 'No' say it like you mean it. When you choose to do a technique, do it like you mean it. Strike through. Go for the jugular. Otherwise, don't do anything at all. To do something half way means you are letting yourself in for serious injury.

Shihan Ron Pickett

Shihan Ron Pickett, Fifth Dan and teacher at Mushin Kempo Karate in Thermopolis, Wyo, has been in Martial Arts for 31 years, and has been an instructor for 25.

"Self-defense is designed to break contact and get away from the attack, not to enter into combat with your attacker. One technique I stress is learning how to escape from getting your clothing grabbed since you are seldom nude when out in public. For example, if someone behind grabs your bra strap through your shirt, this is very difficult to get away from." Pickett teaches self-defense workshops, and stresses, "assertiveness, environmental awareness and physical attacks on a limited number of targets of the anatomy, to inflict surprise, shock or damage. I do not include the groin in this because the groin is too small a target. I use the groin as a last-ditch target."

In his classes, Pickett stresses some key points: Don't make half-hearted attempts at self-defense; make every strike count; each punch must be made with the power of your entire body behind it; worrying about getting hurt during an attack is negative self-talk; don't worry about hurting your attacker; if you are not prepared to do this, you must either give in or run away.

As was addressed earlier, attitude is most important in self-defense. This is an all or nothing proposition. Either be prepared, mentally, to go all out, or don't do anything. In other words, don't threaten anything you are not prepared to back up.

Conquering Fear

David Hein, Sheridan, Wyoming has been in martial arts for 12 years, has been an instructor for six, and has been a police officer for seven. He has taught self-defense courses as well. He talks not only as a martial artist, but also as a police officer. "Self-defense is a mind-set, first off," Hein said. "Most people don't have that mind-set. People have to get the mind-set of not being a victim. They have to think, 'If I find myself in a situation where my life is at risk, I can defend myself.'

"For self-defense, you have to come to terms with the fact that the possibility may arise that you have to defend yourself. You may get hurt, or you may hurt someone."

A lot of people, especially women, don't want to get hurt. Unlike men, who a learn rough and tumble style of play at an early age and collect bruises and scrapes as trophies of their prowess, girls and women seldom do this. I am reminded of the movie *Lethal Weapon*, in which Mel Gibson and his on-screen love interest compare gunshot wounds. I like a woman like her.

For some reason, even if they are being hurt, most women don't want to hurt anyone else. In the book, *The Ones that Got Away*, about battered women, one woman related that her husband was beating her, but she didn't fight back because she couldn't bring herself to hurt him.

I have, in the past, had a hard time with this as well. When someone said something unkind, I didn't want to hurt their feelings by retaliating in kind. Plus, I didn't know how to tell them to quit hurting my feelings.

Through learning martial arts and teaching martial arts and physical self-defense classes, I am learning to be much more verbally assertive. I did not say abusive—assertive. There is a difference. I simply tell people that hurtful comments are not funny and not acceptable. I make it clear to my husband that if he responds to what I say with a sarcastic comeback, I will no longer share my thoughts with him. It is working, slowly. Being verbally assertive also worked several years ago, when a man I took on to help me guide hunters one fall told people that he owned the business, which was mine. I took him aside one day and simply told him to get out. I left no room for discussion. I told him to leave. Anger is a great motivator. I was flat out mad, but I didn't yell and scream. My anger was cold and calm. I knew what I wanted to say, and what I wanted to accomplish. It gave me a feeling of empowerment to know I could handle someone who wanted to basically walk all over me because I was a woman. The man has never been back.

Most women have a problem with the thought of hurting anyone physically. In the book *Armed and Female*, Paxton Quigley relates an experience that happened to her in the early '80s. She was in a self-protection class, and the instructor was explaining the use of Mace as a protection tool. He told them that Mace could not kill or permanently injure anyone. Quigley reports that the women were RELIEVED, because they didn't want to hurt their assailant!

Someone is out to hurt, or maybe kill, and you don't want to hurt them? What about that last mosquito that lighted on your arm for a nibble? Didn't you swat him and think yourself justified? What if a wild dog attacked your child? Would you worry about hurting him if you smashed his head with a baseball bat? See the parallel?

Sure, a human's life is more worthy than a bug or an animal, but only if they give your life the same value and respect. Why should you respect his life any more than he respects yours? Is he better than you? More deserving of life? Are you more deserving of pain. Are you not, as the famous quotation says, 'A child of the universe, no less than the sea and the stars.' Were you not made in God's image as well. Is not your life valuable? In some self-improvement books I have read, they urge people who have low self-esteem to think of themselves as a child that needs nurtured and to provide that nurturing. If you are in a self-defense situation, think of yourself as protecting a tiny, helpless child. Or a puppy. Or a kitten. Fight for them.

Don't worry about hurting your assailant, for goodness sake. HE KNOWS THE RISKS. HE KNOWS HE CAN BE HURT, YET HE CHOOSES TO ATTACK ANYWAY. He chooses to take that risk, he knows the dangers. He is hoping he has chosen well and that you won't give him any trouble. He is counting on it. Like a coyote, who goes for a soft, tender sheep instead of a large, aggressive cow, he is counting on an easy target. Don't give it too him.

Once you have made up your mind to go all out, you will still have some fear. Fear of not being able to do enough damage to stop the attack and fear of getting hurt worse if you fight. There will probably be a moment of panic, of 'I can't really do this!' Panic and fear cause your body to tense, and your brain to cease to function logically. Don't let panic get you hurt.

In Thompson's book, he has an excellent chapter on fear and what happens to the body when adrenaline hits. He also talks of hiding fear. "If you watch a duck it will glide through the water with very little outward movement, however, under the water, where you can't see, his little webbed feet will be going like the clappers. This is how you should learn to control adrenaline. On the outside you should show no signs of the way you feel inside. Very often, if your attacker thinks you feel no fear...he will naturally feel you are not scared. Quite often this will force him to capitulate, after all, no one wants to fight a fearless opponent."

He mentions controlling the various body responses to fear. For leg shakes, Thompson taps a foot. This, he says, gives the impression of being unconcerned. Think about this. Think how unconcerned you look if you are whistling, humming or tapping a foot. It looks that way to others, too. Thompson states that many people become monosyllabic to control voice tremors. If you have ever gotten up in front of a large audience and given a speech, you may have suffered from voice tremors. A trembling voice makes you appear afraid.

Think of being in control and authoritative. I have twice been in a situation of telling men, with guns, that they were hunting illegally on my property. I can't remember my voice trembling; one, because I knew I was in the right, and two, because I was angry. Anger is a great motivator. Be angry, not fearful. Don't think, "Why does he want to hurt me? What kind of a monster is he? Oh no, he'll rape me." Adjust your thinking. Ask yourself, "Who the hell does he think he is to attack me? What kind of a bozo is he? I don't deserve this type of harassment." See how different these statements make you feel? In the first, you are a frightened victim, prey. In the second, you are a fighter, ready to go all out to protect yourself. Practice thinking them.

Thompson addresses two other reactions that you may experience are tunnel vision and the adrenal dump. These often occur in times of high tension and stress. Be aware that tunnel vision can happen, so make a point to keep your eyes moving to avoid being blind-sided.

The adrenal dump has negative affects on the body. It can evoke feelings of helplessness and terror, and may lead to tears and hysteria. Be prepared for this and know it is a normal response to fear.

Peyton Quinn, author and instructor at the Rocky Mountain Combat Application Training in Lake George, CO, has been in martial arts for 30 years, and has been an instructor for 25. He teaches adrenal stress conditioning, a self defense training technology based on conditioning through scenario based training. In an article about Quinn's training in the Jan. 2000 *Black Belt Magazine*, he says that real fights last less than five seconds. Usually the person who lands the first shot wins the fight. In his training, Quinn has men in padded suits yell at the students and use profanity, causing them to experience the heart-pounding adrenal rush that comes in a real street fight, and how to fight in spite of it.

Quinn feels that "many martial arts instructors feel that martial arts training is so closely related to actual self-defense training that they are almost the same thing. This is an error in basic concept that results from most instructor's total lack of experience in actual violence." Quinn's training is designed for defense. "I teach people how to deal with hostile people effectively and the adrenal reaction. Without this, techniques mean nothing," he adds.

When in danger, the body reacts in ways that most of us don't recognize. Freezing is a common reaction to danger. It was a good technique when our caveman ancestors were faced with saber-toothed tigers and wolves, who often depend on seeing movement to determine where the prey is. Today when we face foes that can see us even it we don't move, it has outlived its usefulness. Frozen in fear is more than just an expression; it is a statement of fact.

A friend of mine once had the horrible experience of seeing her cousin hit by a train. The children were playing on the tracks, and the victim saw the train coming, but froze with fear. My friend couldn't pull her from the path of the oncoming freight. Often, extreme fear will cause us to freeze.

Thompson explains it this way: the brain pours adrenaline into the muscles and then has to quickly decide whether to use that adrenaline to fight or run. If the decision isn't made quickly, or if you decide to fight and can't decide which technique to use, the body will freeze while trying to decide what to do. The brain short circuits for a moment, possibly long enough to get you hurt. This is why we stress learning techniques until they are automatic. Then the body can do the technique without waiting for the brain to tell it what to do. It will simply react as it has been trained to do. Think of riding a horse or a bicycle or driving a car. Much of what the body does is automatic, due to years of practice. Self-defense has to be the same way.

One way to learn to control fear is to practice in small, safe doses. Do you freak out at having to give a speech? Practice giving speeches until you have overcome that fear. For one thing, the sweating palms, the trembling legs and voice are the same if you are giving a speech, or confronted by an attacker. Learn to know the feeling and to overcome it through your thoughts, then you will better know how to combat the feeling in a life-or-death situation.

Teach yourself ways of dealing with the fear. Pep talks, (I can do it.), deep breathing, and conscious relaxation are all ways to conquer fear. Very often, if you feel the fear and do it anyway, it is not nearly as hard as you thought it would be. Challenge yourself. Do something that makes your heart pound and your legs weak. Then, if a really dangerous situation arises, your brain will think, "I've been through this, all I have to do is breathe deeply." It really does work.

Controlling the Thought Process

One of the major things that anyone should learn in self-defense is how to give themselves time to think. In one self-defense class, we were taught to simply wait and think for a minute before doing anything. This time is a time to relax, assess the situation, then react.

Although the first course of action, if possible, is to run like hell, this isn't always possible. If you can't, you may have to talk your mind into believing you can handle the situation. Repeating to yourself, "I can handle it, I can handle it," will convince you that you *can* handle it. Panic can be your undoing in a tense situation. Don't panic, act.

I know first hand how the mind can defeat the body. I can spar fairly well in Tae Kwon Do tournaments in my division. Once, as a first degree black belt, I had to compete against the wife of our grandmaster. She herself is close to a master ranking. I was scared to death, knowing that I didn't have the experience to win a match against her. My mind said it was over before I even stepped into the ring. I was whipped before I started.

In any fight, be it in the ring where there is little chance of physical harm, or on the street where the chances of physical harm are great, your mind is your best weapon. Ninety percent of any fight is in the brain. As the above example illustrates, my mind whipped me before my opponent had a chance to try. I didn't even put up a good fight. (I still look back at that and think, "Why? I could have at least tried.") Remember, the mind is still our most powerful weapon in any fight.

Some years ago, some friends and I were having a weekend out at a mountain cabin. I went the night before and spent the night; they would join me later. When I got to the cabin, near dark, I noticed that someone had broken a window and gained access to the cabin. There was no one there at the time, but I wondered, would they come back?

I had choices. I could have left and driven 30 miles home. But I also had a loaded hunting rifle in my vehicle. With that, I decided to stay. Now, I know how to use a rifle, having done a great deal of hunting, and I felt confident I could shoot someone. No one appeared, and I slept soundly through the night. Without the rifle I would have felt less confident.

Today, I would have done the same thing, even without the rifle. There were several good weapons there, butcher knives, a poker for the fireplace, but the greatest weapon is my own self-confidence. I won't allow anyone to hurt me. I am too important.

I would encourage any reader to use the techniques in this book, especially the philosophical ones, but I would also encourage them to enroll in a good martial arts or self-defense class. Ongoing martial arts training is, I feel, an excellent way to contribute to our own personal safety.

Chapter 2

Self-Defense and the Martial Arts

Many women take self-defense classes or martial arts lessons for self-defense. Self-defense classes are valuable in the fact that anything one can take to increase confidence and learn some techniques is good, but the techniques learned have to be practiced.

In an article in the August 1994 *Inside Karate Magazine*, Darryl Caldwell, who teaches at the Oikiasuchou School in Spokane, Washington, says, "It takes skill to be able to pull off the things one would learn in a class, that means practice, practice, practice, practice with a cool head."

A one-day self-defense class designed to only show the techniques is not much use unless the techniques are practiced, and the motivation to use the techniques is there. Without this motivation, even if the techniques are flawless, the moves will be half-hearted and ineffective.

Like painting a picture, you can learn the techniques in an art class, but putting them into practice to produce a beautiful work of art will take a lot of painting.

Practice the movements until they become second nature. If someone grabs you on the street, you should not have to think,

"Which technique do I use now?" You should practice enough so that if someone grabs you, you can react to the threat without thinking.

Caldwell says that during an attack, "One usually isn't in a position to be wondering if he or she is responding correctly. But if one had skills wrought by experience, then one's body would respond automatically."

He quotes an old saying that is very appropriate, "The more you sweat in training, the less you'll bleed in combat."

David Hein puts it this way, "I am a strong believer in conditioning. Nine times out of ten if you can outlast your aggressor, you will win the fight and survive. In my self-defense classes I stress that what you learn may not be effective unless you practice or seek further instruction. Self-defense is more or less specialized. Most self-defense courses incorporate one or more aspects of martial arts."

Hein continues, "After speaking and doing demos in self-defense classes, I encourage students to enroll in a conditioning program and give them a general knowledge of environmental factors."

Most martial arts classes stress conditioning. Even without the self-defense aspect, being in good condition can facilitate either escaping or fighting. When you are in good condition you can run faster and, if necessary, strike harder. In my own case, I have worked for years on a ranch, heaving 70 to 80 pound hay bales, riding horses, and digging post holes. All this adds up to strength training, so I have enough power to hit hard. (In our CPR class, I was doing really good at the heart massage part of the class, until I realized that the cracking sound the dummy was making was because, had he been a real person, I was exerting enough pressure to break his ribs. All of them. Oh well, sometimes we don't know our own strength.)

The Role of Martial Arts In Self Defense

Learning martial arts forms is a way of focusing on the mind and the body working in unison. It gives you an awareness of what your body is capable of. Doing martial arts, I have learned that my left side is stronger than my right side, and that my left roundhouse is better than my right. Whenever possible, I would use my left leg to kick with. I know, through tournaments, what it feels like to be hit, and I know I can live through it—another plus in any self-defense situation.

In my opinion, all women should take up martial arts. It is great conditioning, and in tournament situations women learn how it feels to take a punch or a kick, and how the fighting scene works in a controlled environment. You will feel fear. You will feel the heart-pounding adrenalin rush. Your knees will feel like wet spaghetti. But, you can feel the fear and know you can overcome it. This is a very powerful feeling.

Melissa Horton says of Kung Fu, "The entire art of Kung Fu is a fighting art, and a self-defense art. It teaches the mental discipline necessary to come out of a fight. You need to be fast and have confidence to strike first and strike fast.

"I feel people, especially kids, should get involved in the martial arts," Melissa continues, "It helps to develop individual self-confidence."

Self confidence is gained by accomplishing goals. Martial arts is goal-oriented, with belt rank testings and tournaments. Each step gained is a goal accomplished, and you can look back and think, "I didn't think I could do it, but I did." You have gained self-esteem. One of my greatest achievements is the black belt certificate on my wall. It was a goal I had never thought I could achieve, yet I did. It was a big boost to my self-esteem.

David Hein puts it this way, "Martial arts is a discipline. Through that learned discipline, the mind-set (of not being a victim) can be created and enhanced. It also helps with conditioning and knowledge. Often people are drawn to the martial arts because of the mysticism surrounding it. They want something different. The benefits that can be gained from martial arts: discipline, conditioning, goal setting, carry over into everything one does in life. It is something that you never stop learning.

"Martial arts is very beneficial to youngsters," Hein adds, "It provides positive role models, and reinforces discipline."

Role models are sadly needed today among our youth. Like a stone dropped in a pond, a good role model has a ripple effect. Like Ellen Snortland said in her book, women need positive, warrior-like women to look up to. What better place to find strong women role models than in a martial arts class?

Defining Self-Defense

Sifu Loupos feels that martial arts are a better training field than self-defense classes, "Though I realize some people can derive some benefit from some self-defense workshops I have never favored these activities as a substitute for an ongoing study of martial disciplines. Rather I'm concerned that self-defense courses can instill an false sense of confidence in their participants. Sometimes it's better to be ignorant and justifiably reserved then it is to be confident beyond one's abilities. For the great majority of persons only an extended and ongoing study under a qualified instructor can teach the discipline and develop the resources necessary for real self-defense skills." He added that he hears stories from his students and their parents all the time about how they've used their training to ward off, or more often discourage, assailants and bullies.

We have to be careful of having this false sense of security, but with women I don't see this as a problem. One of my students said her husband voiced the concern that learning self-defense would make her and the other women in the class over-confident, causing them to look for trouble. Unlike men, most women don't go into situations feeling we are supermen. We don't look for trouble; we just want to learn how to avoid it or deal with it if it comes our way.

All self-defense classes are different, all stress different things. In Mike Lovato's self-defense classes, he stresses, in his words, "intensity. I like to make it as real as possible."

Lovato feels that martial arts is not necessarily self-defense, nor is self-defense a martial art. "Self-defense is more direct and more violent. You have to learn it quickly, possibly learn techniques in a one-day class. In martial arts, it is a lifetime of learning, and you learn more than just a few techniques."

Brad Lanka, Tae Kwon Do instructor in Ranchester, Wyo., feels that self-defense and martial arts training is about options. "If you are trained in self-defense, you might decide to take the blows and walk away, or fight back and neutralize your opponent. By taking martial arts and/or self-defense, you have the choice. That's why I train. To have that choice.

"That's what self-defense is all about, taking charge of your life and having the skills to follow through with the choice to fight if necessary."

Brad Lanka feels that a one-day self-defense course could be worse than no knowing anything. "A little knowledge is a dangerous thing. Martial arts and self-defense starts with and is maintained by your own self-discipline."

In other words, you will get out what you put into any training. Practice what you are learning. Even in the basic emergency care classes for first aid and CPR, people who are certified must be re-certified every two years to keep current. You can't just take a course and then forget it and expect it to do you any good. In martial arts, one instructor said you have to practice each form 1000 times for complete understanding. So it should be with expertise in self-defense techniques. They must be practiced.

As mentioned earlier in this chapter, don't ever be fooled into thinking that a one-day self-defense class can prepare you to completely defend yourself. Practice the moves you learn to keep them fresh in your mind. Use the what-if scenarios to decide what techniques would work in what situations. Remember, too, that if the attacker is high on drugs or alcohol, they will not feel as much pain as a normal person. One must strike harder and may have to continue until the person is incapacitated.

All techniques must be practiced in various situations. Punching and/or kicking at a focus pad or a punching bag can help to increase your speed and power. Practice focusing where to hit, and hitting the same spot all the time. Placement can be important. How close do you have to be for maximum power? Practicing on a focus pad or bag can help you find the correct distance, so if the time comes for self-defense, you will know how far away you can be from the assailant to put maximum power in a kick or punch.

In our hapkido class, we practice hand techniques by having our opponents shake our hands. Well, we know that anyone bent on doing damage would not hold out his hand for a shake, but practicing in this way teaches us the correct hold on the hand. The same technique can be used should a man grab a woman by the upper arm.

I asked Master Jae Ho Sim, Tae Kwon Do instructor now of Sioux Falls, SD, if he were to teach one technique in a "crash course" self defense class, what would it be?

"The 'Oso To Gari'" Jae Ho said. "The outside leg sweep. It is easy to learn and very effective." This consists of bringing your outside leg around and sweeping the opponent's inside leg out from under him, while pushing him backwards. Sweeps have to be practiced in close quarters, by grabbing the opponent by the label and the sleeve, and putting your body beside his, while your foot sweeps his foot out from under him.

A friend of mine that I taught this too once took down her husband's bowling partner. She didn't realize that it worked.

The Psychology of Martial Arts

Many people look to the martial arts for self-defense. I am a firm believer in the martial arts. They can be beneficial for several reasons. One, they build self-confidence, the first step in self-defense. Although they don't make you invincible, as even black belts have found out, they do give you the edge.

Martial arts teaches you how to avoid potentially dangerous situations. This is the first step in self-defense. Martial arts, through workouts twice to three times a week, develop muscles and stamina. Anything anyone can do to increase their fitness will help in a self-defense situation.

However, like anything, to get proficient, you must practice. For self-defense, you must also chose the right art. If you are looking for self-defense instruction, avoid classes that merely teach competition or sport karate, especially those that teach students to make only light contact or pull their kicks and punches before impact. This is pretty much worthless as self-defense. For one thing, it helps to spar with someone who is really hitting, even with pads on, to feel a little pain. (We don't want a lot of pain.)

This ability to take some pain is a benefit in a self-defense situation. If you are willing to suffer a black eye, or a bruised shin, or a bloody nose to save your life or your honor, that makes it worth it. Sparring helps to let go of the fear of pain. You get kicked in the shin, and it hurts, but it is not life-threatening. Even a head kick will seldom knock a person out, although it is possible. Still, most can survive it. Knowing what your body can take is a tremendous confidence booster.

Men have the edge here, as many of the sports they engage in include body contact and bruises. Football and wrestling are good examples. Men learn to know their bodies and how their bodies react to pain. Martial arts can do the same for women.

Martial arts also teach humility. I don't believe in bragging about my martial arts. I feel confident that I could use them in a self-defense situation, but I don't feel I have to tell everyone. I also don't want to create a situation where I might have to prove something to someone, so I seldom mention it unless I am talking to friends or if someone asks.

However, in the same breath, I have to say, that as a writer of martial arts books, and to promote those books, I have to maintain a high profile of local interviews, etc. So more people know that I am a martial artist than would otherwise be the case. However, my martial arts are simply a part of what I do. Just like writing, horseback riding, and working. I don't feel the need to brag about my skills, or show them off on the street. That is what my twice yearly tournaments are for. I take the teasing that goes with doing something out of the norm without getting offended. Just like I take teasing about carrying a reading book everywhere, or driving my sports car at 40-plus.

One actor I read about, who often played a rough, tough, take-on-everyone man, was once in a bar, and he saw several people looking at him, looking like they wanted a fight. The actor, who, off screen is not much of a fighter, jumped up and yelled, "Anyone in the place can beat me." He had no more problem.

Chuck Norris has mentioned several times in his two books that people have come to him, in essence, looking for a fight, and he diffused the situation with humor and genuine good will. Sometimes, it doesn't pay to be too aggressive when a "soft answer turns away wrath, but a harsh word stirs up anger," philosophy can work wonders to alleviate a situation. Of course, the Bible also says, "There is a time for war and a time for peace." If your life is in danger, it is a time for war, all out, no holds barred save-your-life at all costs.

According to Robin Buckingham, "Martial arts training is important in that it teaches self confidence and self-esteem, so you don't have a victim mentality. Most people who are assaulted have a victim mentality."

One way to avoid this victim mentality is through training. Ron Pickett sees martial arts or self-defense as a way to learn assertiveness. "By learning assertiveness, you learn not to look like a target of opportunity. Through self-confidence and knowledge that you learn in these courses, you develope a new sense of self-esteem. In a fight or flight situation, you have the ability to make a clear decision. It is wiser to choose the flight choice, but if it is a matter of fight, you will not hesitate in a life-or-death situation."

Pickett continues, "I have taught many government and law enforcement troops self-defense/combat where their skills are tested on a daily basis. The idea of any self-defense or combat situation is best summed up by the acronym that is taught to all instructors, and that is KISS, which stands for Keep it Simple, Stupid. Many instructors go off on a tangent of trying to teach complicated and diversified techniques. To a novice martial arts or self-defense student, this would be the equivalent of putting a child in a room full of new toys and telling the child to pick his favorite toy. The entire idea of self-defense for anyone is to make techniques as simple as possible so the student does not have to train like a full-time martial artist. There are many black belts who train for tournaments only, and when confronted in a self-defense situation either pull their punch or kick, or miss their target completely, waiting for the referee to put their flag up. A housewife would not remember a complicated series of moves, but is capable of remembering anatomical targets. That is why knowledge is power over physical techniques."

Choosing a Martial Art for Self-Defense

Martial arts like hapkido, aikido and judo are good self-defense styles to practice. Hapkido and aikido use leverage and the opponent's weight against them, making them a good study for smaller women.

Aikido

In a *Karate International* article Bob Liedke writes "...Aikido techniques can be used by pressure rather than pain, which makes their use effective even on subjects who can't or don't feel pain because of drugs or alcohol."

Another good point Liedke mentions, and this applies to all martial arts, "You need to train often to become smooth and effective. Unless you have a firm grip on Aikido, you can't use it subconsciously. You need to train until it becomes second nature."

In *Living the Martial Way*, Forrest E. Morgan says that martial artists focus on life, where warriors once focused on death. He adds that today people die just as easily as they ever did, and urges martial artists to train with the thought that combat could mean death. In doing so, he says you will not only train more effectively but live more vibrantly.

Hapkido is another style that favors joint locks and throwing techniques. It emphasizes redirecting the attacker's power and using it against him, and focuses on moving close to the attacker and taking control of the situation. It is an offensive rather than a defensive from of combat.

Hapkido

Jane Hallander in an article in *Karate International* talks about Hapkido as the Great Equalizer for women. She talks about the attacker measuring the distance between himself and the victim, so he will have the maximum power output at that distance. Should the victim move diagonally forward, this will neutralize his force, throwing him off balance and allowing you to take control. Hapkido focuses on disabling the attacker, so he cannot continue the assault.

One of my favorite hapkido techniques is an arm bar. Say a man grabs you by the upper arm, or the wrist. Grab his hand, peel it off you, and with your elbow or other hand, press down on his elbow. He either lets go or his elbow snaps.

Against a bear hug attack, rather than pulling forward, the hapkido stylist will throw themselves backward, knocking the attacker off balance. Or they will grab the thumbs or little fingers of the attacker and bend until they let go. They can follow this with an elbow strike to the stomach.

Judo

Judo, is called 'the gentle art', because it doesn't destroy the opponent. It consists of choke holds, throws, and falls. A woman taking a judo class can learn a great deal about how to react should she be attacked. Jae Ho Sim said, "A lot of women's self-defense courses incorporate judo moves. After blocking a punch or a knife attack, one can follow quickly with a one arm throw, or a hip throw.

"Judo is better for self-defense then Tae Kwon Do, as Judo is a more defensive style, learning what to do to defend yourself, rather then attacking," Sim continues.

In Judo, the student learns to use leverage, and use the other person's weight and strength against him. The two principals of judo are, maximum efficiency with minimum effort, and mutual welfare and benefit. In Judo you can skillfully defeat a stronger opponent by yielding to his attack while maintaining your own balance and throw him off balance.

The first and most important thing to learn in judo is ukemi, or falling. Sim says, "Learning the falls is the most difficult-to protect one's body is one of the most important things to learn." Students learn a front, back and side breakfall, that is how to fall using the forearms and hands as shock absorbers, and keeping the head tucked in to avoid head injury. If a woman learned nothing else in judo but how to fall successfully, she could count the time well-spent.

Learning to fall does several things, it builds confidence, knowing that, should anyone knock you off balance, you can successfully breakfall and come out with little damage. Since most attackers want to get the victim off balance and shake their confidence, anyone who bounces back up from a fall, ready to confront them, has the edge. It also allows the victim, to avoid an injury that could be caused to the head and spine during a severe fall.

I never enjoyed falling, but I did find out that my body was well trained in the art when I slipped on the ice one day and fell. I found myself laying in a break-fall position on the ground, and, except for some bruising on the heel of my hand, I was unhurt. I had used my upper arm to catch my fall, just like I was taught in judo.

Jae Ho Sim told us in one class, "Judo is the toughest to learn and to teach, but once you have it, you remember it for life." Many judo instructors are still doing judo at advanced ages.

"It's all in leverage, not brute force," A 6'2, 340 lbs, instructor told me, when I, at 5'7" and 150, tried to throw him. "You can do it, if you do it right." By the way, I never did throw him, although I could throw some of the smaller students.

In judo you will learn the vital points, where the most damage can be done to an attacker quickly, with little damage to yourself. You will learn how to carry on a fight should it go from a standing situation down to a wrestling situation, as some do. Many martial arts don't teach ground fighting, so that in itself can be a valuable skill to know.

Another important thing about judo is that it teaches pain. You can't learn these techniques without hurting. Most of us limp to class the next day, bemoaning our various injuries and sore muscles. But that too is good, as women often are frightened of being hurt, and this fear leads them to be tense and fearful. Learning to experience pain, and deal with it, gives us that confidence again to say, "well, I got hurt, and it wasn't so bad. I survived that, I can survive this." And, not only survive it, but come back and perform a perfect hip throw on your attacker, bringing him to the ground and allowing yourself time to get away, or hold him until help arrives.

The Benefits of Co-Ed Training

As a self-defense class, judo is good in that the men nearly always outnumber the women. In this way, the women have to work with the men, which is a learning experience. Just knowing that you can and did throw a 340 pound man one day in class using any of the techniques can be a confidence booster. Most attackers on the street look for someone lacking confidence. If faced with an attacker, and you can look him straight in the eye, and think, "I can throw this bozo." This attitude comes through and you are less likely to be attacked.

Self-defense classes where women teach and work with only women are lacking something. A woman should work with men to know how much larger and stronger they are, and what techniques to use. Darryl Caldwell says, "Women-only classes, where there are no men, are playing dangerous odds in that a woman needs to practice on a male body..." He adds that the men should not be husbands, boyfriends or relatives, as they often just humor the woman, giving her no idea if the techniques really work.

Unless you train with men, you don't know where the best places to strike might be to cause maximum damage, or how a man reacts to pain. An elbow strike on a woman with no abdominal conditioning would be different from doing the same strike on a man who has developed his stomach muscles. An armlock on a man with a thickly muscled arm will require a much stronger technique than on a woman whose arm is smaller and more delicate.

Kathy Wilson, instructor in the Kyukido Martial Arts School in Casper, Wyoming, puts it this way, "I think women should train with men. Otherwise, you don't know your strengths and limitations. You have to find out if you can do the techniques on a man-sized target. You won't know where your limitations lie unless you practice the techniques."

Most men, on the average, are taller and stronger than most women. Thus, to successfully do an elbow strike to the nose, one would have to reach higher, and may not even connect with the nose. In the December 1997 *Tae Kwon Do Times*, Scott Kelley, Jr., wrote, "Unless a woman is skillfully trained with years of experience, she probably wouldn't have much chance of escaping the grab of a large man."

This is a good point. Don't expect a weekend self-defense course, a year of martial arts training, or even a black belt, to make you invincible. Like playing a piano, writing publishable articles, kicking a football, or riding a horse, to become proficient you must practice. Sure, its boring, tiring, and not always fun, but without practice, you really can't expect the techniques to work.

There is an excellent article in the July 1992 issue of *Black Belt Magazine* titled "The Element of Surprise" by Anthony J. Pallante. In it he uses a real-life example of a brown belt who fell victim to an aggressive drunk. The martial artist assumed he could just step outside and finish the fight. The drunk, using the element of surprise, attacked while the man was setting down his beer on the bar, and was the victor of the encounter. So don't get overconfident of your skills. Unless you know for sure you can handle your opponent, you are best to walk away if at all possible. If this isn't possible, then be prepared to use the quickest, hardest technique you can to disable your opponent and get away.

Realistic Practice

Techniques should be practiced on someone wearing street clothes, including a heavy coat. An elbow strike, to be effective through a heavy leather coat, would have to be much harder than the same strike through a t-shirt. Grabbing a gi in judo is different that using the same move against someone without a shirt, or attired in a tight fitting t-shirt.

A woman should also practice in street clothes. Practice in the dojang, then practice wearing your usual clothes. Kicking in high heeled shoes or heavy hiking boots is different from kicking in bare feet. Even tennis shoes are heavier. Also, with shoes, the striking surface may be different than in bare feet. Hiking boots may make it difficult to get the foot into a good position for a round house kick. Cowboy boots with a formidable heel, lend themselves to side kicks with the heel leading. (I always feel sorry for anyone in the movies who gets kicked by someone wearing cowboy boots. Even though I know it's fake, I think how it would feel in real life.) They are also excellent for stomping insteps.

If you wear skirts, practice in a skirt. A loose skirt presents no problem and a split skirt would be much like a kendo master's large pants. However, a tight, short skirt would make kicking difficult.

Elvis Presley's wife took karate from Chuck Norris, and she asked him to teach her wearing her high heels and skirts. A good idea: If that was the clothing she wore every day, it was the clothing that she would be wearing should she be attacked, and the clothing she would be wearing when defending herself.

Kicking in tight fitting pants is more restrictive than in the loose fitting pants of the gi. In the winter, wearing a heavy jacket will make arm techniques more difficult. Practice techniques in all clothing, so you will know how they function in every situation.

Mike Lovato, who stresses realism in his self-defense classes, comes in occasionally to my classes to teach us new techniques. One night he let us use him as the uk (partner who gets thrown or takes a fall), and he "attacked" us, letting us find our best techniques. It was an interesting experiment. Some of my students found that techniques that work on still bodies, don't work as well on someone who is always moving and trying their best to knock you down and possibly destroy you. Much like a real attack, in these simulations, the adrenaline is flowing and movements are fast. Everything is speeded up. Try it sometime on a partner who will, without hurting you, keep attacking until you have successfully defended yourself.

Martial arts and self-defense take dedication and practice. Self-defense in particular takes determination and a willingness to survive at all costs. Quinn said about his RMCAT training, "I can take a group of Navy Seals and teach them to fight hand to hand pretty easily and have done so. The real challenge is to take a passively socialized housewife and in a weekend teach her to avoid, defeat or kill a would-be rapist. I've done that too and find that the much greater satisfaction."

Chapter 3

Weapons: Pro and Con

A word about weapons: knives, guns, sprays, stun guns, etc. all have their place. But, like an expensive camera in the hands of a three year old, to get the proper results you must know how to use the weapon. To give someone without any training an expensive camera and expect Ansel Adams quality photos is useless. Sure, they may get lucky, but most of the photos will wind up in the round file.

Like any self-defense technique, weapons require training, skill, and practice. Robin Buckingham says, "Unless you train with weapons a lot they don't do much good. They can give you confidence, but you have to be prepared to use them. You must practice constantly to become proficient."

The worst mistake people make with a gun is thinking that the gun itself will create fear in the criminal and cause them to back off. Not always so. It is said that one should never point a weapon at anyone that you don't mean to kill. That doesn't mean that you should kill every time you point a weapon at someone, but it does mean you have to be prepared to kill. Don't ever think that a gun will scare someone into leaving you alone. Most criminals can tell if you intend to use the weapon or not. Make sure if you have a gun, and know how to use it, that you are prepared to shoot, and shoot to kill if warranted.

Once, many years ago, our house was robbed while we were at work. The deputy we called apprehended the suspect, but he called for backup, and I took the only hunting rifle we had left, a 22-250 loaded with hollow points, to help the deputy as he cuffed the man. I held the rifle on the guy, and the deputy said, "If he moves, shoot him." Looking down the gun barrel, which was less than a foot away from his shoulder blades, I told the guy I'd shot a lot of other varmints and I wasn't about to miss him at this distance. He didn't move a muscle as the deputy put the cuffs on him. Later I heard that he glanced up at the deputy and his eyes were as big half-dollars. For about a year I was the talk of the Sheridan County Sheriff's department.

This illustrates that I was, at least in his mind, prepared to kill him if necessary. One has to be strong in purpose, and let the criminal know it. Had my voice quavered, which it didn't, or had I seemed at all unsure about shooting, this would have revealed itself to him. As it was, I came across as very deadly. For one thing, in a self-defense situation, WE DON'T KNOW HOW FAR GONE THE ASSAILANT MIGHT BE. Anyone under the influence of drugs could be pretty far gone, and attack anyway. Be prepared.

In the movie, *Sleeping with the Enemy*, Julia Roberts is confronted with her abusive ex-husband. She is holding a gun on him. He is trying to talk her out of killing him. She dials the police, and he feels he's safe, until the dispatcher answers and Julia Roberts says, "Hello, police, I want to report a murder." Then the husband knows that she means to kill him then and there.

The whole point is, weapons can save your life. Peyton Quinn said, "Weapons are always the first choice. The gun and knife are the most useful. But, like unarmed techniques even these are useless if adrenal conditioning is not in place."

Anyone using a weapons has to:
1. Learn how to use them, and learn how to be a responsible gun/weapon owner.
2. Have them loaded and within reach if a confrontation occurs.
3. Know the laws regarding them.
4. Be prepared to use them.
5. Use them only in life or death situations. Even police are often brought up on charges if they fire at the wrong moment, if a life wasn't threatened.

In *Empty Hand, Loaded Gun,* Dan Westerlin brings up the following points on using a gun as a weapon: He uses the scenario of finding an unarmed burglar in the house. You have a handgun. No one is in danger of death or bodily harm, but if you introduce a firearm to the situation, according to the law, you can be considered the dangerous party.

In every situation, Westerlin says that the reaction has to fit the situation. You have to make sure that you react strongly enough to avoid injury to you, but not so strongly as to commit the mistake of killing someone who wasn't that dangerous. In this same vein, I once read about a policeman who shot a young boy who pulled a toy gun on the police officer. Talk about a major mistake. I wouldn't want to be in the policeman's shoes for anything. Would you?

Brad Lanka stated, "When you send out energy in any weapon, be it empty hand, bo-staff or gun, you have to be willing to live with the consequences of that action. Anyone using a weapon should be trained to use the weapon or it's no good."

Weapons and Safety

All in all, in today's society, weapons are often either kept by the bed unloaded (who is going to wait for you to load a gun?); kept in a purse, (difficult to find during a moment of stress and fright); or in the hands of someone untrained to use them properly. This last fact is the reason that some homeowners are killed with their own guns. They are not really prepared to use them. They hope for a bluff; but we can't depend on the other person buying that bluff. If they don't, we are left with the choice of killing them, and if we are not prepared to do that, we can lose the battle and the gun can be taken away and used against us.

One big argument against guns is that children have been shot while playing with guns. This is a real concern. But the way many of us in this area grew up was that there were always hunting rifles around, (for one thing, we used them against varmints, rabid skunks, coons in the chicken house, injured animals, etc.) Kids were taught to LEAVE THEM ALONE and we did. I can't remember of any incident when I was growing up of a kid shooting anyone with a family gun. Parents taught responsible gun handling and ownership. If there is a gun or guns in the house, this is what should be done.

Children should be taught the proper way to handle and fire a gun, and taught to leave them alone unless they are with their parents. We were always taught, as children, to respect toy guns, and to never, never point them at another person.

Knives are a good way to start teaching children to handle weapons responsibly. Children can use knives with supervision. As they prove they can use the knife correctly, they can carry pocket knives. Growing up on a ranch, we were taught to use knives and guns, but we knew and were taught to use them responsibly. At 12 we were allowed to hunt prairie dogs, and today my son, Paul, has been hunting on his own with a .22 and shot gun since he was 12. At 15, he is trusted to take a ranch vehicle into the hills and shoot prairie dogs with a .22 rifle with his cousin. However, I know both boys know guns, and are responsible. If a boy I didn't know wanted to go, I would make sure an adult was around until I decided that the new boy knew how to use guns.

Even as a girl, I learned to use guns at a young age, and my daughter, although she doesn't hunt big game, knows how to shoot and enjoys target shooting.

A friend of mine was at one time, when she was around 12, left in charge of the house overnight while her folks went to town. (This was in the mid-1900s, and trips to town could take awhile with the horse drawn wagons that were still in use in Wyoming). My friend said, "I slept with a shotgun under my pillow. Later our hired hand said, 'Boy, I'm glad I didn't come into the house unexpected.'" One thing, if a child has a gun, how does the attacker know if he can use it or not. The attacker may reasonably wonder if the kid is going to get scared and just start throwing lead around. Most kids today have grown up on cartoons, where a bad guy can get shot and get up and walk away later. Depending on the age, kids have little concept of death. They usually won't be afraid of killing someone with a gun, because they don't make the connection of death. I'd be scared to face down a kid with a gun, just in case.

Owning a gun is a responsibility. It cannot just be purchased, set in a drawer, and only brought out if you perceive a threat. You have to be responsible about the fact that you own something that can kill. I am not anti-gun. I have guns and know how to shoot them. But I realize that, like the old saw in playwrighting, "If a gun is seen in the first act, it has be used by the third," if a gun is brought into play in a situation, you must be mentally prepared to fire and kill if necessary.

Seriousness of Intent

Once, in our small town, two men got into an argument in a bar. One man went to his truck and returned with a gun. He told the other man, "Stop, or I'll shoot." The other man kept walking, and he wound up dead. (The man with the gun wound up in jail, but the fact remains, he was prepared to shoot and did so.)

Ask yourself, if a man threatened you, you had a gun and he continued to walk toward you, could you and would you shoot? And would you be willing to face the consequences? If you bring in a gun, do not let it be turned against you. But be very sure that your life is in danger and that deadly force is the only way to stop the confrontation.

In Bruce Tegner's book, *Complete Book of Self-Defense*, he writes, "Anyone who kills, even in self-defense, has to live with the consequences for that action for a life-time. Killing, even in self-defense, must ordinarily be justified through a trial and court."

Knives or edged weapons are good defensive weapons, IF ONE KNOWS HOW TO USE THEM. Knives are a weapon that can be easily turned against the defender, if they are not prepared to strike fast and hard. As the swordsman said in *Chapter 1*, "be prepared to cut and die." In other words, go all out. Don't threaten with the knife. Be prepared to just use it. Quickly.

I love knives, often write about then and love to collect them. My favorite is a small push dagger that is a replica of those used in the Old West by gamblers. It is small, easily tucked in the hand, and, if used properly, can be deadly. However, because it is small and flat, unless I carry it in my hip pocket, it resides in the bottom of my book bag. Not terribly handy in case of an emergency. There again, have your weapon handy and readily available.

One should learn to make do with what weapons are close at hand. If you have a gun, say, that is in the bedroom, what good is it if you are confronted in the kitchen? Look around, what can be used as weapons in each room? In Thompson's book he quotes knife expert Peter Robins as saying, when talking about a knife which can be used for utility purposes as well, "What turned it into a weapon was the person using it."

This is true of anything that is used as a weapon. It is not so much the weapon used, as the intent to use it.

Sprays and Stun Guns

In the defensive tactics for personal defense class, the instructors recommend such items as key-ring pepper sprays, which are small and handy. However, one has to be very close to do any good. In an interview with a self-defense instructor in South Dakota, she said one woman had a can of either pepper spray or mace, but it was in her purse, <u>still in the plastic case.</u> If you purchase a self-defense weapon, have it ready at hand.

Small hand-held electric 'stun guns' are being sold as defense weapons. I have one small 'zapper.' According to the box, mine packs 65,000 volts, is of compact size, and is a "legal electronic device that puts out a high voltage shock. By merely touching a person with the stun gun, he is immobilized for several minutes with no permanent damage."

The energy stored in the stun gun is dumped into the mugger and causes the attacker's blood sugar to be converted to lactic acid so his body becomes unable to function. Holding the gun on the attacker from "1/2 to one second, will startle the assailant giving him some pain, muscle constriction and shock; one to three seconds will cause muscle spasms and a dazed mental state; three to six seconds will cause loss of balance and loss of muscle control."

I accidentally was on the receiving end of a zap from my small stun gun. I can personally attest to the startle, pain and shock effect, and I doubt that I touched it for half of a second. My family said they have seldom seen me move so fast. I can say that the shock hurt. Badly.

As far as doing any nerve damage or causing confusion or loss of muscle power, I didn't sit still long enough to find out. I likened it to a hornet sting, and it made be want to get away from it FAST.

Sheriff David Hoffimeyer of Sheridan, in speaking of the electric shockers that the police use said, "They work for what we do." If a person can get to them, and get them onto the person assaulting them, I can see where they would probably give a person time to get away. However, depending on the attacker, it might just make him madder. Use your own discretion in using one. If I had one, and had no other choice, I would attack the face, throat and other tender body parts. Then it may be very effective. Also, don't think you're going to scare someone by saying, "I have a zapper." If the situation warrants it, it is better to have it in a coat pocket, so you can strike hard and unexpectedly with it.

Again, the problem is getting to it in time to do any good. The one I carry is encased and in my bag which I carry everywhere.

Pepper sprays could be effective, judging by the eye watering pain that cayenne peppers give when you accidentally rub your eyes after cutting them up for cooking. Unlike the zapper, you don't have to make physical contact, but you do have to hit directly in the eyes. These should be practiced with (on an inanimate target, not another person) to make sure you can direct the spray properly, and be capable of judging the distance needed.

Pocket guard 'zapper'. Good for a quick shock value, but one has to be close to use it.

A canister of pepper spray. Pepper spray is designed to be sprayed into the eyes, which will cause extreme burning and watering of the eyes, allowing one time to run away.

Woman's Best Friend

For home self-protection, a dog is a very effective deterrent. Even a small dog will bark at an intruder, giving you time to call the police. A large dog is a good deterrent: most burglars or people looking for an easy mark will hesitate entering a home when faced with a large, ferocious looking dog.

I have always had dogs, usually large ones. A friend of mine is noted for not being afraid of dogs, and can usually walk into anyone's yard, right past a barking dog. Somehow, she intimidates the dogs. I had a dog one time who knew the lady, and would still not let her in the yard. It was a half-wolf, very protective, and she said it was the only dog she hadn't been able to intimidate.

Other Views on Weapons

The instructors I interviewed had differing opinions on weapons.

David Hein said that there are three major categories of effective weapons. "Firearms are first. OC spray, which is a powerful pepper spray, is second, then edged weapons such as knives. Anything else is moot. Stun guns are not very effective, especially through clothing. Plus, you have to get close enough to touch your assailant with it. Pepper spray has a range of about 10 feet."

Other professionals carry pepper spray. In our BEC class, the instructor said he was called to a scene where many of the bystanders were drunk and hampered the ambulance crews attempts to help the injured parties. "I thought once I would have to employ my pepper spray to break up the crowd," he told the class.

Pepper sprays are also recommended for hikers as a way to deter grizzly bears. If it will stop a grizzly, it will sure stop a human.

I asked each of my interviewees about weapons and found many of the answers were similar. It didn't matter what the weapon was, it was the intent behind the weapon which made the difference.

Sifu Loupos says, "Weapons for self-defense are a tough call given the litigious society we live in today. However, weapons training encourages students to think creatively and learn adaptive skills. If you can use a sword you can use a tennis racket, if you can use a knife you can use a hairbrush."

Ron Pickett pointed out the same thing. "Anything that can be used as a weapon in a self-defense situation should be used. The idea of self-defense is for you to defend yourself by any means possible. If you lose the advantage, you may also lose your life. In my seminars, I teach a variety of weapons that most women have available in their purse. The one tool I teach that is an intended weapon is a kobuton. It is a stick that is usually used as a keychain that under federal guidelines is defined purely as a defensive weapon. The kobuton techniques can be used with a variety of readily available things, i.e. lipstick holder, toothbrush, pen, tampon. In my seminars I break boards and bricks with a tampon without damaging it, just to prove a point." I saw a demonstration video that Pickett and his class put together, where Pickett broke a board with one finger. That was impressive.

Simple household objects can deliver a powerful blow.

A kubotan can be used to cause pain in the soft
areas of the body, such as the throat.

As Pickett and Loupos said, anything can be used as a weapon. A rolled up newspaper or umbrella can be used to poke to the solar plexus (the spot under the breastbone.) A hard poke will knock the wind out of a person. One man, a fencing champion, once used his umbrella as a sword to defeat a mugger.

Keys or pens and pencils placed between fingers act like brass knuckles if one throws a punch.

A cane is a good all-around self-defense weapon, easy to carry, legal, and very deadly in the right hands. In the September 1998 issue of *Tae Kwon Do Times*, Jimmie Nixdorf talks of his cane defense. "A cane is both practical and legal." He writes, "It is an item commonly used by many people, and it is almost always at their disposal."

He points out that for defense purposes, a cane is technically a club. But while clubs are illegal in many states, a cane's "primary function is to assist the mobility and visually impaired."

A cane can be used for striking, for blocking, and for throwing and trapping. It has long been taught as a weapon in many Korean styles. A cane can be thrust into the solar plexus area, or at the throat. The hook can be used to hook the ankle, knee, elbow or neck. A person with a cane can hook an attacker's elbow with the cane, then proceed to do an arm bar, or hook the neck and follow with a punch.

Keys between fingers act like brass knuckles, but be prepared to hit hard and get away. In a dangerous situation, strike for the eyes.

When I was a kid, my grandfather always had his shepherd's crook cane right next to his chair. He would tease us by gently hooking our ankles as we went past him. Being a large, tough ex-rancher, I'm confident that he would have used that cane to his advantage if he had ever been attacked.

To use a cane requires very little physical strength, so it is a good weapon for elderly people, who should learn to use their canes as defensive weapons, if the need ever arises.

Even Kyokushinkai Karate founder Mas Oyama wrote, "A gentleman must regard his walking stick not only as an ornament, but as a defensive weapon to use on his own behalf or on the behalf of others in danger. Practice these stick techniques because they may be of considerable value to you in the future."

Not many years ago, I trained for awhile with a friend who was a fan of Modern Arnis, the Filipino art of stick fighting. Although I never pursued it, I did learn quite a bit of good stuff. I liked the techniques of using the stick, with strikes to the neck, ribs, knees and head. These can be used with sticks, swords, open hands, or such weapons as a cane and umbrella. Some of these will be included in the techniques section.

As with any form of self-defense, the choice to use a deadly weapon such as a knife or a gun is a personal one, but one that should be looked at from all angles. One should be trained to use the weapon, and trained to think before using it.

Like Miyamoto Musashi, who was reputed to have killed and disarmed several sword-wielding opponents using only a wooden sword, if one wants to maim or kill badly enough one can do it with anything. Knives, books, pens, wooden sticks, even hands and feet, if properly trained. It rests more in the mind of the defender than in what weapon is used.

Chapter 4

A Special Message to Parents

In the book *Yes, You Can Say No* Manuel J. Smith, PhD. writes, "Socially, young kids sometimes behave like sharks. Sensing another child's vulnerability, as sharks sense blood, they attack that child verbally. All of us know what a good child is. A good child is a people pleaser - more specially an authority pleaser."

Teaching children to be good children leaves them little room for independent judgement, something they need to maintain a healthy self-image and ego.

Smith goes on to say that parents teach their children to be good children, but do not teach them to handle social conflicts. Good children, he adds, often can be readily talked into misbehaving, truancy, cheating, and later into sex and drugs. In the book Smith gives several examples of how youngsters can be verbally assertive without being aggressive.

In looking in our local library for books to reference to on teaching children how to say no and how to protect themselves, I found very few. Most were concerned with ways to teach children to be good. One is titled, *Children who Say No, When You Want Them to Say Yes*. Another is concerned with how to break the will of a strong willed child without harming the spirit. There are many books on how to parent to raise children who don't talk back, who don't threatened a parent's authority and who do what their parents' say. Somehow, I found the selection discouraging. Where do children learn when to say No to an adult who might molest them? Where do we teach them that they have boundaries over which no one should cross?

These are important parts of child-rearing as well. We want children to feel confident that they have control over their bodies, and that no one can touch them in places that make them feel uncomfortable. We must also let them know that if such a 'bad touch' occurs, we, as parents, can be trusted to make sure it never happens again. We have to convey to our children that we will protect them, and that we are teaching them to protect themselves when we are not around.

I can remember vividly as a child, being told to "beware of strangers and not take candy from strangers." I was literally terrified until I was about 10 or 11, of even 'talking' to a stranger. I think this is very much overkill. Would I have even asked a stranger for help if I had ever been lost? I doubt it. It is my thought that when a child is very small, up to school age, that parents have the responsibly to know where that child is at ALL TIMES, who they are with, and what they are doing. Just a minute of inattention can lead to fatal results.

Some things parents should do, even for very young children, age 3 and up, is to teach them their full name, their parents' names and phone number, including area code, their full address, as well as how to dial 911. They should also teach them how child molesters and kidnappers operate, how they can sound convincing by using phrases like, "I have a puppy to show you." or "Help me find my cat." A parent should go over with a child some ways to say no, ways to help a child recognize a potential threat. There are good books on the market with different play-act scenes for parents and children.

Once, many years ago, my younger sister, who was about six or seven, was dropped off at the local library to look at books or for story hour. We lived some forty miles from the town, not uncommon in Wyoming, and we were in Sheridan for the day.

With Linda at the library, my folks were delayed. The library was getting ready to close. My sister knew her name, which was little help as we didn't live in town. We didn't have a phone at the time, so our name was not in the phone book. Linda didn't know the full name of her aunt May, who lived not far from the library. Luckily, one of the librarians knew someone named May, and it was the correct one. But had it been a larger town, (Sheridan was about 10,000 people at the time) my sister would have been completely lost. The friendly librarian called my aunt, and soon Linda was reunited with the family.

Where I live is very rural and everyone usually knows everyone, and we watch our for each other's children. Since everywhere, even towns 10 miles away are long distance by phone, memorizing the area code is simply a part of the phone number. However, until recently, the only address many of us had was a post office box. This isn't much help if someone has to find a house in an emergency.

A Child's Options

In a situation where a child is being attacked by an adult he/ she has several advantages. Children are smaller, they can hide in places an adult can't reach, like under a car or in a culvert. Children can learn to throw rocks and keep an attacker at bay by pelting them with rocks. They are lighter, and can climb higher in a tree due to their smaller size. Children have to be taught to use their advantages, including the element of surprise. Seldom, unless they are very well trained, can a smaller, weaker child do much damage to an adult.

They should be taught how to protect themselves against their peers as well. When my boy was about 9, he was being picked on by an older boy. As Paul had completed some karate training, I told him to use it if necessary. I also told the boy's mother I had given Paul permission to use what he had learned. Later, the boys became, if not friends, at least not antagonists.

A good book on the subject is *Protecting our Children From Danger*, by Bob Bishop and Matt Thomas. It has a lot of tips and techniques for children, parents and self-defense instructors.

Children in other periods of history were more self-assured and more able to take care of themselves than most children today, although many inner city youths learn to live on the streets at a young age.

In earlier eras, young boys ran away and became cabin boys on ships; rode for the Pony Express; or became cowboys on the long trail drives. Young girls became mothers at 14 and 15, and learned to run households.

During the early days of the industrial revolution, children in Europe were many times the sole support of their families as they worked in the textile mills and coal mines. Some were younger than 10. In 1848, Pennsylvania enacted a law saying that children under 12 could not work in certain mills and limited hours of work to 10. Although I don't think we should go back to this, I am pointing out that children can be given a great deal of responsibility, and are very capable of taking care of themselves. I think today's parents should try to foster more of this independence in their children. We have to protect them, but we won't be around forever.

If they learn independence and self-protection young, it will follow them throughout the rest of their lives.

Chapter 5

Techniques

Geoff Thompson, a self-defense instructor and bouncer from Great Britain, featured in the Oct. 1999 issue of *Black Belt*, talks about how to handle a 'gratuitous aggressor,' or someone who instigates an ego-based confrontation stemming from accidental situations. He defines three types of attacks: match fight, where the combatants agree to fight; the ambush, or surprise attack; and three-second fighting, or as he puts it, "a real-life street fight involving the three C's - confrontation, conflict and combat." The second two scenarios are the most likely to occur in a self-defense situation. In either of these instances, avoidance should be the first line of defense.

Avoidance Tactics

Thompson describes a fence tactic, using the hands to create a physical barrier between the aggressor and the defender. "Placed correctly the lead hand will not only maintain a safe gap, but will also nullify your aggressor's weapons, such as punches, elbow strikes, head butts and knee thrusts." The fence, Thompson says, also acts as a sensor to the aggressor's intentions, and a range finder, to allow you to judge the exact distance for a preemptive strike.

Another point Thompson stresses is using dissuasive dialogue for "loopholing." "Loopholing means giving your adversary an honorable way out of the situation so he doesn't lose face," Thompson says.

Although self-defense wasn't involved, I once did this unconsciously. We have barbed wire fences and it takes a certain knack to open the gates. I once had a hunter who, after straining with the gate, watched open-mouthed as I used the technique and opened the gate quickly and easily. He was a weight lifter and was very put-out that I had showed him up in front of his buddies. "It's all in the technique," I said. Giving him that out, that he wasn't weak, just unknowing. He saved face.

Another time I was guiding when I found a man trespassing on our land. Even though he tried to talk his way out of it by saying he was an 'old family friend,' I told him to get out and not come back. I did this to his face, but not in front of the friend he had along. I also allowed him to take the deer he had killed and I didn't turn him in. By not embarrassing him in front of his buddy, I allowed him to save face. Even though he got somewhat aggressive, I had three hunters with rifles in the back of the pickup, so the trespasser left without any real problems, but it might have been different if he would have had to 'prove something' to another hunter.

Thompson adds that posturing is one way to avoid a confrontation. Posturing is a matter of convincing your opponent, by your actions, that you are, indeed, someone who will fight, and might just hurt him. He advises creating a wide gap between you, perhaps with a shove and a leap backwards. He also advises, once the gap is created, pacing side to side aggressively, never taking you eyes off the aggressor.

Watch an animal to get a feel for this tactic. There is a lot of posturing in the animal world. A dog will often do this with another dog to show that he means business. Cats, too, posture a lot before a fight, showing off their size and strength. Often, posturing can create confusion and self-doubt in the adversary, allowing time to make your getaway.

Posturing is a matter of not backing down. It says, "I'm willing to go all the way."

Like when I chased off the trespasser: he knew I wasn't impressed by his 'old family friend' routine. He was posturing, trying to convince me he had a right to be there. I didn't buy it. I did know him, but to call him a friend was a wide stretch of the imagination. He saw that and knew that I was willing to chase him off at gun point if necessary, so he backed down and left.

When I'm working cattle, I posture by waving a stick or jumping in front of them to head them off. They don't know that I will give ground if they don't stop. This is posturing, as is stepping in front of a horse that doesn't want to be caught, and blocking his escape route. He could charge over the top of me, but I make him think he can't.

Posturing is very much a part of sparring. We fake and feign kicks and punches to allow us to get the opponent in position for the real kick or punch. Practice this in a martial arts class and it could come in handy sometime on the street. Thompson says, however, that by posturing you give up the element of surprise and deception. If the aggressor decides to attack, it can become a match fight.

In a tournament match, we're taught that if you do a fake, then do it with as much power and conviction as you would a real technique. In that way, if your opponent doesn't move, you can follow through and use the technique. So, if posturing, be prepared to follow through.

Keep it Simple

In *Dead or Alive, the Choice is Yours,* Geoff Thompson has some excellent advice on self-defense. For one thing, though most attackers are looking for a weak, pliable victim, they are usually cowards at heart. And remember, the would-be assailant knows nothing about you. You might have a gun. You might be trained in fighting arts. You might have a bowie knife and know how to use it. Therefore, as Thompson states, 'when ignorance is mutual, confidence is king.' Confident people are very rarely chosen as victims of an attack.

If you have ever played poker against a seasoned player, you will realize the importance of a good bluff. Many times people lose at poker, not because of the other fellow's exceptional hand of cards, but because of the other fellow's exceptional skill at bluffing. If you watch animals, you will see many times that animals are great in the use of bluff. Don't be afraid to do the same.

Some teachers, emphasize doing one technique. "Learn one technique and learn it well," advises third-degree black belt Brad Lanka. He feels that self-defense is not a one-size fits all, but that techniques are individual and have to fit the person using them. Sometimes, if you have too many techniques, you will waste valuable time trying to decide which technique to use. If you have one you know will work, use it.

Robin Buckingham uses a slightly different approach, "I teach three to four moves that women can learn to boost their confidence level. I never advocate sticking to only one technique." She teaches three or four so you have back-up techniques. Say you depend on a block, grab, and elbow break. What do you do should your attacker come from behind and grab you in a bear hug or a choke hold? This is a valid argument for learning a variety of techniques.

Thompson agrees, "....perfect one or two techniques. Make them, via conscientious practice, your own. Practice until you develop power and accuracy." He also addresses the advanced martial artist in saying that one should, "...choose your strongest technique and make it stronger, work it until it is absolutely natural and comfortable."

Sifu Loupos says that although he does not have one technique that he favors for self-defense, he added that, "...if the situation is serious enough to warrant it, striking an opponent's knee is quick and easy and can facilitate escape (and very good for women.)"

The best tactics follow the K.I.S.S. principal: Keep It Simple Stupid. In a self-defense situation forget the high flashy kicks. Kick low, to maintain balance. Kick for the knee; taking out a knee is taking out the foundation. Knees are fairly weak and from the front or the side they can be easily broken or dislocated with the right kick.

Mike Lovato teaches "... simple, straightforward techniques which require little thought or practice. Use the EENT approach, eyes, ears, nose or throat, or a good hit to groin." He added that this approach is easy to learn and takes little thought. "In an attack, you normally have seven seconds to react. You can't spend time deciding which technique to use. You have to act fast and forcefully, be 'swift, silent and deadly."

That makes us sound like snakes: swift, silent and deadly. I like it. I use this approach in my classes. The eyes, ears, nose and throat are nearly always available as targets, even in winter. Most people will instinctively protect their eyes and in doing so will open up other targets.

In speaking about his police training David Hein states, "In law enforcement, most of the techniques we use are empty hand techniques, arm bars and wrist locks. We very seldom draw our firearms, but we use empty hand techniques on an everyday basis." He recommends, "A kick to the shin or groin, and a wrist lock or arm bar if someone grabs you. The ultimate goal is to get away. Escape. You don't have to stay and fight."

Any technique should be done quickly, using the element of surprise, and with determination. Thompson says it very well, "People often ask me what is the best means of physical defence, and I always reply, 'Learn to hit ****** hard.', and that is the bottom line." The attacker may want to kill you. Why should you hold back?

"Ninety-nine times out of 100, the first strike wins," Lovato says. "You have to depend on instinct. Most of the time you can tell when the situation has gone the limit, and when it is time to strike."

This goes back to using your institution and listening to your inner voice so you know when to respond.

Side kick, taking out the ankle or knee. Good,
quick, effective, easy to learn.

Hand Techniques

Learning to kick is good, but you should also learn techniques for close-in fighting. Kicks are useless at close range. In an article in the May/June 1997 *World of Martial Arts*, there is an article titled *Women and Self-Defense, the Total Approach*, by Michelle Fauquier. In it she quotes Dr. Thomas Nardi, clinical psychologist and black belt. Nardi states, "...the ever popular kick to the groin is actually too dangerous a technique for women to use in a real self-defense situation..."

He explains, "...men instinctively protect the groin area, and anticipate that women will kick to this target." An attacker can then grab a woman's leg and dump her to the ground. The ground is the last place a woman wants to be during an attack. "..they (women) would do better to focus on the so-called poison hand techniques." Poison hand techniques are open-handed strikes to extremely vulnerable areas.

The web hand. Taking throat between thumb and first finger. Effective if done quickly and hard.

Strikes

Eye pokes, spear hand strikes, and palm strikes are better than punches. They are quick, effective, and don't require a lot of strength. Go for sensitive areas, eyes, knees, groin, tops of the feet, throat.

Eye Poke

To execute an eye poke, take your first two fingers and make a V. Think about the distance between your eyes and spread the V accordingly. The fingers should be slightly bent, but ridged. It sounds gory, but the fingers should be stiff enough to go into the eye sockets, if necessary.

Spear Hand

A spear hand is a good technique to perform a thrust to the solar plexus area. Your hand should be flat, the fingers pointed out away from your body. Your thumb should lay along the top of your hand. For the most power, the hand should be chambered next to the body and when you thrust, you should thrust with power and speed, and then pull back. It should be a quick, sharp thrust.

Palm Strike

A palm strike to the nose can send an attacker backwards, cause bleeding and pain. The eyes will water and for a moment it will take the attacker's breath way. A palm strike to the chin can send the attacker's head backward, and can cause whiplash to the neck. In a palm strike the hand is held facing up, with the heel of the hand slightly forward. This is the striking area. The fingers should be slightly bent. Again, chamber the arm for maximum power.

Knife Hand Strike

For the knife hand strike, or the traditional karate chop, the hand is held away from the body, palm up, with the outer edge of the hand slightly elevated. The strike is usually used against the neck, and should hit the neck with force, while swingng slightly upward at the same time.

For the reserve knife hand, the hand is palm down, and the strike is thrown from the inside of your body. Take your hand in the palm down position, and lay your thumb against your neck. Swing the arm outward. Striking area is again the outside of the hand. With all strikes, strike through the target. Don't just hit the throat and stop, hit as if you are hitting the wall behind the attacker.

Elbow Strike

One of the best defensive techniques is an elbow strike. Executed correctly, an elbow strike can disable an attacker, create an opening for a series of other techniques, or give you time to get away. The best strikes are those at the attacker's bony body parts: the jaw, ribs, solar plexus and temples.

An elbow strike to the solar plexus will knock the wind out of someone allowing you to get away. An elbow strike is great in close quarters when you can't kick or punch. They are also effective in that the attacker can't kick or punch so well either if you are close enough to use an elbow. Elbow strikes are better than punches in a close situation.

Web Hand

A real quick, simple technique is a web hand, one that Lovato teaches in his self-defense classes. Take your hand, spread the thumb out and put the fingers together, forming a half-way lazy L. This can be used to strike the throat quickly and hard. Not life threatening, but enough to stop the opponent, even if he has you on the ground.

Hammer Fist

A hammer fist is as if you are pounding on a table. Think of a hammer driving a nail. Use the bottom part of your fist.

Back Fist

A back fist or a hammer fist is better than a punch. A back fist is a strong swing with the back of the hand, bringing the force to bear from the inside of your body. Hold your fist, fingers curled in, thumb on the outside of your hand, against your chest, thumb against your chest. Bring your hand from your chest straight out from your shoulder.

The backfist is an effective strike when you are close to your attacker and have one or both arms free to strike with.

Other Techniques

Collar or Lapel Grab

If the attacker grabs you by the collar, or the arm, trap his hand with you opposite hand. If he grabs your right arm, use your left hand to grab his hand and hold it while you take your right hand, cup it under and slightly behind his elbow. Push his arm up, breaking the joint elbow if necessary. Make sure your hand is under his elbow, you want to force the elbow joint against the natural curve.

Choke Holds

If being choked with an arm around your neck, turn your head to see where the attacker is and to take some of the pressure off your throat, and then align your heel with his leg, sliding down his shin and stomping on the instep.

A one armed throw could also be used if the attacker has an arm around her throat. Grab the arm, step sideways away from the attackers elbow, bend down, using the hip to push into the attacker, and pull him over your shoulder.

Other choke hold escapes consist of a thumb grab, bending the thumb back, or bending the little fingers down, will both cause the attacker to let go. But these are not crippling moves. This should be followed with an eye gouge or a hard slap to the groin or a palm strike to the nose.

Oso To Gari, or leg sweep, could be used if an attacker grabs a woman by the front of her shirt, trying to force her down. To do this technique, grab the attacker's shirt, slide your body sideways, hook his leg with the heel of your foot, drive your hip into his back, and sweep his legs out from under him. This technique is almost impossible for an untrained attacker to deflect or defend against.

Kicks and How to Use Them

Side Kick

A side kick is straight out from your side. This can be effective on ankles and knees. Hit with the side of the foot. The striking area is the side, or blade, of your foot. A side kick is good to aim at the knee if someone has a hold on your arm or is standing beside you with an arm around your shoulders.

Front Kick

A front snap kick is good in some instances. Bring your knee up and snap your leg out, hitting with the ball of your foot. This is a good kick should you wind up on the ground, or if someone is bending over you when you're seated.

Again, strike through. Kick at the knee as if you are trying to go through it and hit the other leg as well.

Kicking to the leg or knee can unbalance your
attacker and give the chance to get free.

Stomp Kick

A stomp to the instep is like stomping a really ugly black bug. Stomp heel first for maximum force. This is a good move if you wear heeled boots or high heels; not as effective if the attacker is wearing heavy hiking boots.

The best bet too is to strike hard and fast, then run. Get away. Don't wait around to see if he is moving again, or don't try to finish him off. Just hit hard and fast and leave.

Techniques should be practiced. Practice hitting and kicking at a punching bag or ball suspended on a string to learn accuracy and speed. Try taking one look a the target and then try to hit the target when looking away. Another way to practice is to have a friend help you. Wear a blindfold and have your friend snap their fingers. As soon as you hear the sound, simulate a blow aimed at the source of the sound. Assaults are more likely to occur in dark place than in lighted places. Practicing blindfolded helps to concentrate your defense on the sound. In this way you will be less likely to panic if you can't see your opponent.

Practice with a partner, using focus pads for speed and power and reaction time. You can also practice strikes at the body, without hurting your partner. This is where working with a well-padded partner will benefit. If you train in the martial arts, maybe your school has a training mannequin that you can practice aiming your techinques for maximum damage.

Targets

The human body has several places where a strong blow can cause injury, pain or death. Anyone interested in self-defense should take some time to learn these nerve centers and become familiar with them. An excellent book on the subject is *Nerve Centers and Pressure Points* by Bruce Tegner. In the book he also elaborates on the pain that can be caused when using the techniques on a larger, smaller, and equal-sized partner. As bullies usually attack those smaller than themselves, I have concentrated on what happens when the technique is applied by a small person to a larger person. Of course, the larger and stronger the person doing the technique, the more powerful the technique will be.

Buckingham teaches a lot of pressure point techniques in her self-defense training. "Nerve strikes work, drugs or not. It may take more pressure on a drunk or someone on drugs, but nerves will work." She adds that, "Self-defense is an automatic response. You can't think about the technique during an encounter."

Solar Plexus

The solar plexus, located under the breast-bone, is a good target for an elbow strike or a fist. Even if the attacker is larger, a forceful hand blow or elbow strike can cause pain and could affect breathing for a moment. There is a tiny bone at the end of the breast bone called the xiphoid process. In BEC we learned that breaking this bone during chest compressions could cause lacerations of the liver and internal bleeding.

Nose

The nose is an excellent target. For one thing, although much of the body may be covered by heavy clothing, the nose seldom is. Even a face mask is no protection. A forceful blow to the nose will hurt, causing watering eyes and considerable pain. However, unless the fighting is very close, it is not advisable that one step in close JUST TO HIT THE NOSE. When possible, stay out of range.

Eyes

The eyes are an oft-mentioned target area for an extreme defensive measure. Again, this is in-fighting. Techniques such as eye jabs and eye pokes should only be used in life-threatening situations, as the possibility of serious injury to the eyes is very likely, no matter who is performing the technique. If the assailant is wearing glasses, sometimes simply knocking the glasses off will cause momentarily disorientation.

Chin

A blow to the chin can jar the head and snap it back, a heavy blow can knock a person off balance, and even induce unconsciousness. Again, this is a close-in tactic.

Throat

The throat area is very vulnerable. A moderate blow can cause gasping and choking. A heavy blow, even from a small person, could be fatal. A forearm blow or a knife hand slash can be used on the throat. The hollow of the throat is very vulnerable. Control of someone who is annoying or offensive but not threatening great harm can be achieved by placing a thumb into the hollow of the throat and applying slight pressure.

Knee

A strong kick to the side of the knee will unbalance the assailant and possibly lay him out on the ground. A kick to the front of the knee may injure ligaments and/or dislocate the kneecap. This is a good target no matter what the size of the assailant. A kick to the back of the knee will most likely result in buckling of the knee and bringing the attacker to the ground. A good kick to the knee is a side kick.

Shin and Instep

Both the shin and instep are sensitive to hard strikes. A forceful blow from a smaller person will cause pain. A good technique is a hard kick to the shin, followed by scraping the foot down the leg and stamping on the instep with as much force as possible.

A hard side kick to either the ankle, calf or Achilles tendon will cause extreme pain to the opponent.

Depending on the season, some targets may be covered with heavy clothing, thus unavailable. Anyone wearing heavy, high topped work boots is less likely to experience pain when kicked in the ankle. The knees, however, are nearly always a good target, as even the warmest clothes do not offer sufficient protection against an attack to the knee.

Heavy coats make the solar plexus a difficult target to hit accurately and forcefully. Try for the throat, nose and eyes.

Blocks

Practice blocking techniques. Blocks are used to stop a punch, and give you time to hit back.

A forearm block is simply a movement to deflect a punch, or a grab. Make a fist and hold your arm at a 90 degree angle. Bring your arm to your chest, and then bring it out. Think of someone swinging a fist or a ball bat at you. Push it away.

A high block is designed to protect your head. One good way to practice is to have someone work with you using soft, spongy encounter backs or Nerf bats. As someone tries to brain you with the soft bat, bring your arm up to protect your head. Arm is bent at about a 45 degree angle, held about six inches from your head. The bend of the arm allows a bat or stick to slide down the forearm. With a high block, you can protect your head, and see your assailant, and possibility counter with a strike of your own.

A well timed block can deflect your assailant's arm and
prevent him from getting a good grip on you.

Escapes

The Kyukido Federation has several good, solid techniques for escaping chokes, hugs and grabs.

Hug Escape

The assailant hugs you face to face but leaves your arms free. With one hand on his chin, the other behind his head, quickly snap his neck. Our instructor wrote a warning on this, "DANGER! Be very careful not to hurt your partner while practicing this technique. Completion of this technique could cause death."

Another possible escape from the front hug is a knee strike to the groin.

Arm Grab Escape

Another effective technique if someone grabs your arm is the arm bar. Take their hand, applying pressure on the sensitive area between the second and third knuckles. Peel off the hand and execute an elbow break. Of course, you don't have to actually break the elbow. Using the opponents weight against him, simply swing him around and bring him to the ground. From there you can execute a head kick or a face kick.

In hapkido we practice hand techniques, and as Brad Lanka says, "Hapkido is a 30 degree twist and 30 degree lift." You twist the hand 30 degrees and lift it 30 degrees for maximum pain and leverage. If your hand is grabbed, twist it to bring the thin part of your hand around to loosen the grip is very effective. Once you twist his hand, he is somewhat off balance, and by twisting you can get the thinner part of your hand in a better position to pull away, especially if the attackers palm is sweaty, or your wrist is slick.

To practice this escape, have someone grab your wrist. Twist your hand and discover how it is nearly impossible for the attacker to hold on to it. Don't, however, pull backwards and spread your fingers, this makes it easy for him to keep a grip.

When grabbed by the wrist, first twist out between the thumb and first finger . . .

then pull up and away to escape.

Collar Grab Escapes

Another technique can be used if an attacker grabs your collar from behind. Turn to face your attacker, while at the same time bringing the arm closest to the attacker up and around, like the blade of a windmill. Then bring it down sharply on his arm above the elbow.

Pushing up on the elbows of someone grabbing you. This is an another effective technique for escaping from a front grab. A hard upward push can dislocate the elbow.

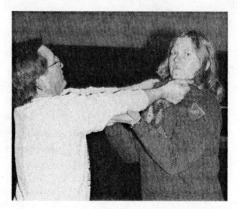

Escaping Against a Standing Assailant

As the assailant grabs her clothes, she aims a side kick at his knee and/or his stomach.

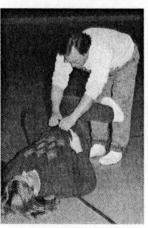 

Ground Pin Escape

Slap the assailant's ears between the hands (like clapping) can cause extreme pain and a broken eardrum. Never practice this on a partner because it can cause an injury even if done with less than full power.

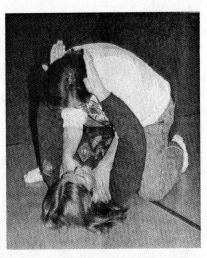

Hair Pulling Escapes

When grabbed by the hair, a palm strike can be used a close range and kick to the knee can be used if the attacker is at arm's length.

Finding your Best Techniques

There were some techniques I found in another self-defense book that, when tried in a training situation, did not work. One of those is the one that demonstrates when someone is sitting on your stomach, bring your legs up and grab him around the neck. I tried this several times and, unless you are very athletic and/or your legs are very long, this does not work. I guess this is one argument for keeping very limber.

My personal favorites are the arm bar, the under-the-elbow break, the one armed throw, Oso to Gari (leg sweep), the side kick to the knee, and the neck break.

Take some self-defense training. Although books can help, nothing can replace really doing the techniques and doing them properly. A good instructor can help you to learn the best and easiest way to execute the techniques, and show you how to put them into practice. Find those you like and that you feel you can successfully execute on another human. Practice them in a number of different situations, in the gym, outside, in street clothes. Tight jeans make kicking difficult. Just because someone promotes a technique, doesn't mean it is the best for you. Read and talk to people about the difference between the way a man attacks another man and the way he will attack a woman. There is a big difference. Find techniques that work best for these type of attacks.

We also must learn to react automatically. Walking and driving require many motor skills, but once learned these habits are automatic. When driving a stick-shift, one must push in the clutch, shift the gear, give the motor some gas, let out on the clutch easy, and then (hopefully) the vehicle starts smoothly. This is repeated every time the vehicle needs to be shifted. With practice, it becomes automatic. One way to become automatic is to practice, and master the basics.

Chapter 6

Scenarios

As the first line of self-defense is the mind, here are some ideas to get your mind in the self-defense mode.

Much of self-defense is common sense. Don't go into dangerous situations. Park in lighted areas. Stay away from places where alcohol is served. Over and over, in interviews, I heard self-defense instructors say, "I don't have any success stories of people who used techniques. They avoided the situation before they had to use the techniques."

David Hein echoed this. "Anyone with the self-defense mind-set learn not to put themselves in dangerous situations, so they will not have to use the techniques."

This is what we strive for. Here are some suggestions:

Travel Safety

1. When traveling, learn about your car. Learn how to change a tire and keep your vehicle well serviced to avoid breakdowns.

2. Keep the gas tank at a half tank or better. In this way you will be less likely to need help from some stranger who might not

have your best interest in mind.

3. If you break down and someone offers to give you a ride, ask them to call the highway patrol instead.

4. When traveling alone, let someone know where you are going, your estimated time of arrival, and where you plan to spend the night.

5. Call home when you reach your destination to let them know you are okay. If you are going to be late, call and let someone know. Get in the habit of keeping in touch with friends or family. That way if you don't call in, they will know that something has happened.

6. Listen to the weather forecast and consider canceling if a bad storm is predicted.

7. Carry enough money or use credit cards to 'hole up' in a motel should bad weather catch you on the road. Icy roads, blizzard conditions and strong winds can make driving hazardous.

8. In bad weather, too, avoid taking scenic back roads and know exactly where you are going. About five years ago, an elderly lady took a wrong turn on a very isolated back road, mistaking it for a better traveled secondary highway. She got stuck in a muddy ditch, and spent several days in her car, staying alive by melting snow and eating snacks, until she was rescued. In a place were evil people might have been lurking, she may not have survived.

9. If you are traveling alone, don't stop to help stranded motorists, call the highway patrol when you find a phone and report the situation.

10. Don't pick up hitch hikers.

Self-Defense in Real Life

Carrying a gun when traveling alone might be a thought for many. My cousin, newly discharged from the service many years ago, once picked up a hitch hiker who drew a knife on him, saying, 'What would you do if I told you to give me your car?"

"I'd to this," my cousin replied, drawing a pistol from under his seat and pointing it at the man. They rode in mutual distrust until my cousin dropped the man off and went on his way.

11. When walking along a road, face traffic. It is more difficult to pick up someone who is facing traffic than who is walking with traffic. For one thing, when walking away you can't see behind you. Walking with traffic allows you to keep the cars in sight.

Mental Practice

To prepare yourself for any contingency, write down several scenarios you may find yourself in. What would you do in each one to diffuse the situation, to defend yourself if the situation escalates, and how do you escape? It is said that the mind cannot tell what is real and what is imagined. Therefore, if you imagine enough ways of getting out of a situation, your mind will be programmed, like a computer, to take over and remember what you did to save your life "the last time" even if saving your life was all in your imagination.

Think about as many as you can, no matter how absurd they may seem. Visualize what you would do, visualize your opponent leaving, running away, being taken down by you and laying on the

---

Self-Defense in Real Life

Once when my mother and I were hauling a trailer load of cows to the sale barn, the major belt in the pickup broke. Stranded on the roadside, we were looking over the situation when a man in an old car stopped and asked if we wanted a ride to the gas station about 30 miles down the road. Although he was probably okay, I said, "No, but if you would call the highway patrol or a wrecker in Sundance we would appreciate it."

About an hour later, a wrecker appeared and put the belt in for us and we were up and running again. Was the man okay? Would he have gotten one of us safely to the next town? Probably. But I was not willing to take a chance that he wasn't a decent human being. (His bumper sticker, with a reference to Satan, might have had something to do with my reluctance.)

pavement while you run away.

In our black belt test, we had to 'defend' ourselves against several attackers. This is a good practice to give you an idea of what to do if you are attacked by several people. Think of a scenario with several attackers, and think how you will get away. Think about where you would kick, punch or strike if necessary.

Here are few scenarios to get you started:

Scenario One

Your car is in a dark parking garage. Getting your keys out of your purse, you are grabbed from behind with an arm bar around your neck. He is threatening you with dire harm. You....
  a. Panic and struggle?
  b. Turn your head to allow breathing space in the crook of his elbow while you think.
  c. Stomp hard on his instep?
  d. Bring your fist up and connect with his nose?
  e. Grab his arm and throw him over your back?
  f. Grab a finger and bend it back to make him let go?
  g. Elbow strike to his stomach?
  h. Kick him in the shin?
  i. Scream? Use bad language? Tell him to let you go or else?
  j. Stab him in the eye with your car key?
  k. Bite his arm?

Your best choice would be b. Think about your situation. For one thing, it calms your panic and allows you to consider your options. Is his nose in a position where you can do a hard, confident back fist? Is he wearing a heavy coat, making an elbow strike less effective? Can you grab a finger? If so, then what? Can you grab his arm and effectively throw him? Is he wearing tennis shoes, while you're wearing boots or heels? Try for the instep. If he's wearing work boots and you have on sandals, your power to hurt is diminished. If you can reach his eyes, go for it. Or bite him hard on the arm, ear or nose.

If there is anyone you think might hear you, scream for all you're worth. Cuss out your aggressor. In the book *Armed and Female*, Paxton Quigley, quotes a convicted felon at the California State Penitentiary who advised women to use foul language. "These guys are all used to hearing bad talk. We've been talking bad all our lives. We don't know any other way to talk."

Scenario Two

You're sitting in your house, when someone knocks on the door. You're expecting a friend, and you open the door only to find a man with a knife. He forces his way into your home, threatening you bodily harm. You...

(Living room)
   a. Grab the ugly table light your granny gave you for Christmas and bash in his head?
   b. Grab the telephone and smash him in the face.
   c. Grab a picture off the wall and jab the sharp corner of the frame in his eye. Once, in an abusive relationship, my sister-in-law cold-cocked the guy with a picture, cutting him severely with the glass. He had to have stitches.

(Kitchen)
   a. Grab a skillet, same technique as lamp, only more effective. Nothing beats a cast iron skillet when it comes to knocking someone colder than last night's bean soup. Aluminum works okay, but not as a well as good old cast iron. It isn't as heavy, and it dents easily.
   b. Grab a rolling pin, same technique.
   c. A wine bottle also makes an impressive club, but don't waste good wine unless absolutely necessary. Use an empty and save the full one for celebrating.
   d. Grab the sink sprayer, give him a good douse of hot tap water. (Although, with a sink like mine, he would actually drown in cold water before the hot water got there, but if his eyes are full of water, he still can't see to hurt you.)
   e. You could grab a butcher knife, just make sure, for intimidation purposes, that it is a bigger knife than the one he has. Be prepared to use it. Of course, to use a knife, one has to be within arm's length. If the attacker has a knife, do not let him get close enough to use the knife. If you have a knife as a defensive weapon, strike hard and fast: don't let the knife be taken away and used against you.
   f. Glasses, vases and plates make good weapons. Throw the entire set at him. Unless they are expensive China, you can replace them.

g. Chairs can be thrown as well. Just make sure you have good aim, so it can't be thrown back.

h. Household cleaners squirted or thrown into the eyes can cause anything from pain to blindness.

Scenario Three

Same as Scenario Two, except he has a gun.

One thing to remember, according to Debbie Leung in *Self-Defense, the Womanly Art of Self Protection and Care*, an attacker usually carries a weapon to "...coerce the victim into meeting his demands, rather than to injure the victim." An attacker who makes

---

Self-Defense in Real Life

Once, I heard about a fencer who was set upon by a knife welding mugger. Using his umbrella, and several fencing moves, he defeated the mugger. What sports or hobbies do you have that could contribute to your survival? A good pitching arm could come in handy throwing rocks. Martial arts training teaches kicks and punches. Any active person, who routinely works at jobs such as construction, ranching, or even housekeeping, will be more conditioned than a person with a desk job who lives life as a coach potato. Any person with active, aggressive hobbies, even tennis, horseback riding, training large dogs, jogging or whatever, will come out better in a confrontation, if they fight, than a sedentary person.

But many sedentary hobbies have defensive weapons. The old saw about hat pins is true. When close enough, grab a knitting needle and go for the eyes or the throat.

Have animals? Holding a cat when confronted by an assailant could be a bonus. A cat can be thrown into an assailant's face, giving one time to get away.

A dog is a great alarm and defense weapon, the bigger and meaner looking the better. I have even heard of attack rabbits and attack chickens. I always felt a large python would be a great crime deterrent, or even the tarantula as in the movie, "Home Alone".

demands and threatens to use the weapon if his demands are not met is probably using the weapon for coercion.

Remember, EVEN IF THE ATTACKER HAS A WEAPON, don't panic. Think. Many times assailants DON'T KNOW WHAT TO DO if the victim is not afraid of the weapon. This puts them off balance, and may be long enough to give the victim a chance to use a self-defense technique to disarm the assailant. You may be scared to death, and your knees might be trembling violently, but as long as you can convince your attacker that you are not scared, it could go a long way towards saving your life.

I once heard that a threat was golden as long as it worked. i.e., "I will shoot you with this gun, so do what I want." The threat becomes tin if you are not intimidated.

When faced with a gun, which has a greater distance, of course, than a knife, never panic, and never give up thinking. If there is a place to go, run. Most people who use a gun for intimidation, can't shoot.

Sometimes waiting works. If rape is on the assailant's mind, he will undoubtedly lay down the weapon at some point. Use this juncture to your advantage. If you strike, strike hard and fast to disable the assailant. If you know how to handle a gun, and have to opportunity to get it, do so.

Keep your mind clear and keep thinking all the time, looking for an opening.

Robin Buckingham put it very well, "The most important thing in self-defense is never give up, and give it all you've got,"

Scenario Four

A man comes up and orders you out of the car at gunpoint. The window glass is between you.

　　a. If you can, gun the motor and leave the area. Even if he shoots, the chances of you getting hit by the bullet while you are moving are fairly slim, and you have a better chance than if he is able to get inside the car with you.

　　b. If you can't drive away, and are in a busy area, honk the horn.

　　c. If the window is open, and the assailant shoves a hand

inside to grab for you, roll up the window on his hand.

d. If a man forces his way into your car, drive erratically and hope someone calls a cop. If you are belted in, a hard stamp on the brake may project him through the windshield. Remember, if you are driving, you are still in control of a very deadly weapon, your car. Just because he says, "Do as I say and you won't get hurt," don't believe him.

If you are driving the assailant probably won't shoot you for fear of killing himself should the car run off the road. "An attacker is unlikely to want to attack the driver of a car whilst it is in motion because he is as likely to get hurt in the subsequent crash as the driver." Thompson writes in *Dead or Alive*.

You could also make a beeline for a police station, if you know the area, or drive up beside a police car. I would make sure I kept moving, probably at a high rate of speed, that means no stopping even for stop lights. Stay in populated areas; the further from people, the more danger you could be in.

Practice these and other scenarios asking yourself, "What would I do if this happened?"

Chapter 7

Overcoming Fear

A friend of mine, a very large woman but normally not aggressive, was once in a crowded bus depot when a man grabbed her by her long braid. Turning, she began cursing him in language learned for years from her father, a professional boxer. The man, stunned, said, "Okay, lady, okay. I didn't mean any harm." She one time even took a rifle away from a hunter who was hunting illegally on her property. She told me, "My father taught me to not be afraid of anything."

Feeling fear and making it work for you is one principal of self-defense. Don't be fearful for nothing, like the heart-pounding rush of a ghost story. Why do these frighten us? Why does even the thought of ghosts frighten us? Ghosts are immaterial, and can't hurt us, yet more people get shivery about ghosts than about real fears. Like the fear of ghosts, much of fear is illusion. We have to learn to let go of fears that are based on illusion, and concentrate on real fears.

We want to live without fear, but in a state of alertness to protect ourselves. First, by avoiding dangerous situations, and second, by having the confidence and courage to protect our lives and the lives of our loved ones at all costs. Remember the caribou; be ready to draw blood in your attacker. Be swift, silent and deadly in protection of yourself. You are important. You have to live.

We have to train the spirit as well as the body, so that during times of crisis there will be complete emotional and mental clarity. We have to love life. Accept life. Face life. See life. Engage Life. Instead of training, like the samurai, to die, we train to live and stay alive. Live each moment and see things as they really are, without judgement.

Bibliography

Tales and Strategies from the Jade Forest and Beyond, 1994, John C. Loupos, Jade Forest Press, Cohasset Ma.

The Gift of Fear by Gavin De Becker (1997, Gavin de Becker, Dell Publishing Co., New York.)

The Woman's Way, Time-Life Books, Alexandria, Vir., 1995.

U.S. Department of Justice, Federal Bureau of Investigation, Washington, DC.

Dead or Alive, The Choice is Yours, Geoff Thompson, Summersdale Publishers, West Sussex, UK., 1997.

Rape Awareness and Prevention, Robert and Jeanine Ferguson, Turtle Press, 1994.

LA Law Enforcers catalog, Yakima, Washington.

Protecting Our Children From Danger, Bob Bishop and Matt Thomas, North Atlantic Books, Berkeley, CA.

Armed and Female, Paxton Quigley, St. Martin's Paperbacks, 1990.

Self-Defense, the Womanly Art of Self-Care, Intuition and Choice, Debbie Leung, R&M Press, Tacoma, Wash., 1991.

Beauty Bites Beast, Ellen Snortland,

Nerve Centers and Pressure Points by Bruce Tegner. Thor Publishing, Box 1782 Ventura, CA. 93001. 1968, 1980.

Yes, You Can Say No, Manuel J. Smith, PhD. 1986, Arbor House, New York. and Institute of Systematic Assertiveness Training and Human Development.

Bruce Tegner's Complete Book of Self Defense, Thor Publishing Company, Ventura, CA., 1977)

December 1997 Tae Kwon Do Times, Scott Kelley, Jr., in an article "Women (Martial Artists) are Different."

Instructors Guide to Teaching Women's Self-Defense Seminars, Brian J. Olden, Turtle Press, 1998,

The Secret Power Within, Zen Solutions to Real Problems, Chuck Norris, Broadway Books, New York, 1996.)

Women in the Martial Arts, edited by Carol A. Wiley, North Atlantic Books, Berkeley, 1992.

Karate International, July 1992, Bob Liedke article, "The Incredible Martial Art of Aikido")

Safe Homes, Safe Neighborhoods, Stopping Crime Where You Live, Stephanie Mann with M.C. Blakeman, 1993, Nolo Press, Berkeley.

Protect Your Home and Family, Ted Schwarz, Arco Publishing, 1984, NY.

Parenting for Prevention, How to Raise a Child to Say No to Alcohol/Drugs, David J. Wilmes, Johnson Institute Books, 1988, Minneapolis, MN.

The Ones Who Got Away, Women who Left Abusive Partners, Ginny NiCarthy, Seal Press, Seattle, WA, 1987.

In Defense of Ourselves, Linda Tschirhart Sanford and Ann Fetter, A Dolphin Book, NY 1979.

Empty Hand, Loaded Gun, Dan Westerlake
U.S. Department of Justice, Washington, DC, 1998

Sources

Special thanks to the following contributors:

Melissa Horton, instructor at Jade Forest Kung Fu, Rapid City.

Robin Buckingham is a third degree black belt in Taekwondo in Rapid City, SD and instructor at the ATA Black Belt Academy.

Sifu Loupos, Jade Forest Kung Fu Academy, Cohasset Ma.

Shiran Ron Pickett, Self-defense and martial arts instructor, Thermpolis, Wyoming

Bill Kipp, RMCAT, Lake George, CO

Geoff Thompson, bouncer, author, self-defense instructor,West Midlands, United Kingdom

NRA Women's Issues, 11250 Waples Mill Road, Fairfax, VA 22030

David Hine, police officer and martial arts instructor, Sheridan, Wyoming.

Mike Lovato, self-defense/martial arts instructor, Clearmont, WY

Master Jae Ho Sim, martial arts instructor, Sioux Falls, SD.

Matt Ford, police officer, Sheridan, Wyoming.

About the Author

CV Rhoades has been training in martial arts and self-defense for eight years. She has trained in Kempo, Hapkido, Judo, Tae Kwon Do and Modern Armis. She is currently teaching a woman's self-defense class in her hometown of Clearmont, Wyoming. She feels that the mind is the most important part of self-defense, and self-defense and martial arts should train the mind as well as the body.

She holds a black belt in Tae Kwon Do through the American Kyukido Federation, and is continuing to train at the Sheridan Martial Arts and Sports Academy under Mr. David Hine.

She has written two other books, including *Strike Like Lightning, Meditations for Martial Artists,* also from Turtle Press, as well as several articles. She is currently enrolled in the Refuse to be a Victim Instructor program through the NRA, learning more about self-defense training methods.

Also Available from Turtle Press:

Muye Dobo Tongji
Martial Arts After 40
Fighter's Fact Book
Warrior Speed
The Martial Arts Training Diary
The Martial Arts Training Diary for Kids
Teaching: The Way of the Master
Combat Strategy
The Art of Harmony
A Guide to Rape Awareness and Prevention
Total MindBody Training
1,001 Ways to Motivate Yourself and Others
Ultimate Fitness through Martial Arts
Weight Training for Martial Artists
Launching a Martial Arts School
Advanced Teaching Report
Hosting a Martial Art Tournament
100 Low Cost Marketing Ideas for the Martial Arts School
A Part of the Ribbon: A Time Travel Adventure
Herding the Ox
Neng Da: Super Punches
250 Ways to Make Classes Fun & Exciting
Martial Arts and the Law
Taekwondo Kyorugi: Olympic Style Sparring
Martial Arts for Women
Parents' Guide to Martial Arts
Strike Like Lightning: Meditations on Nature
Everyday Warriors

For more information:
Turtle Press
PO Box 290206
Wethersfield CT 06129-206
1-800-77-TURTL
e-mail: sales@turtlepress.com
http://www.turtlepress.com

Printed in the United States
51363LVS00002B/103-204

9 781880 336540